SHAMELESS

SHAMELESS

REPUBLICANS' DELIBERATE
DYSFUNCTION AND THE BATTLE
TO PRESERVE DEMOCRACY

Brian Tyler Cohen

Foreword by Jamie Raskin

HARPER

An Imprint of HarperCollins*Publishers*

HarperCollins books may be purchased for educational, business, or sales promotional use. For information, please email the Special Markets Department at SPsales@harpercollins.com.

FIRST EDITION

Library of Congress Cataloging-in-Publication Data has been applied for.

ISBN 978-0-06-339288-5

24 25 26 27 28 LBC 5 4 3 2 1

To Grandpa Bernie.
The world was a kinder, gentler,
more patient place with you in it.

In this hyper-polarized, highly charged era, when trust and the truth are hard to come by, it's been especially rewarding for me to find myself at the forefront of a burgeoning and crucial independent media ecosystem.

However. Getting to the heart of this Republican Party's dysfunction—in all its nuance, complexity, and stupidity, and with an eye to precedent and stakes—requires the help of experts. It would be immensely challenging for anyone to try to understand, let alone explain, our political landscape without conversations with and contributions from, ideally: a historian and professor; an international journalist and head of an independent media company who has become an authority on holding power to account; a preeminent constitutional scholar who is a sitting member of Congress; a renowned voting rights attorney; a former White House press secretary who is a news host on a major television network; a senior communications advisor to President Obama who excels at dissecting our political landscape; a member of President Biden's Cabinet with first-hand experience of campaigns and a vision for the promise of America; and a former member of the U.S. Senate—preferably one who wrote for *SNL* and later penned a bestseller about how *Rush Limbaugh Is a Big Fat Idiot.*

As I am none of those things, it was my great honor, and it is this book's great fortune, that the following experts were kind enough to sit down with me to discuss their opinions, insights, and forecasts. This book would be significantly less informed if not for their generous contributions.

So, very special thanks to Pete Buttigieg, Marc Elias, Al Franken, Mehdi Hasan, Dan Pfeiffer, Jen Psaki, Jamie Raskin, and Heather Cox Richardson.

CONTENTS

At a time when every monstrous political ideology and toxic hatred from the last century has been revived and released into our politics and media ecosystem—with some new hallucinatory pathologies and Artificial Intelligence dangers thrown in for good measure, the searching young voice and unwavering decency of Brian Tyler Cohen have appeared like a sparkling diamond in the political rough of the internet.

A self-made podcaster, commentator, and internet agitator, Cohen pursues an old-fashioned agenda that would be instantly recognizable to Tom Paine. He expects essential fairness and justice from our political institutions and demands the truth from political actors. His passionate connection to the civilizing movements and freedom heroes of our past is utterly refreshing and redeeming, just as his disdain for authoritarian propaganda, disinformation, and corruption is irresistible and inspiring.

This book reads like a quick-witted travel journal Cohen has kept on his voyage to challenge the resurgent enemies of democracy and to organize the contemporary friends of freedom. He pays close attention to the structure and mechanics of government along the way, and explains the specific process reforms that will enable us to break out of the matrix of anti-democratic institutions and practices that the forces of MAGA thrive on: the gerrymandering of our legislative districts, voter suppression tactics, money-soaked elections, and right-wing judicial activism enabled by right-wing court-packing.

Through his odyssey, Cohen brings back good tidings and revived common sense. Ringing in our ears at the end of this book is a voice of uncommon integrity and political purpose—reasonable, passionate, and urgent.

—*Congressman Jamie Raskin*
April 15, 2024

SHAMELESS

CHAOS IN THE CHAMBER

Alabama congressman Mike Rogers, face flushed, beelined to Matt Gaetz and lunged toward him, his index finger pointed at the Florida lawmaker's face. Sensing a fight, another Republican congressman, Richard Hudson, came up behind Rogers, grabbing both his shoulders and ultimately palming the irate lawmaker's face in an attempt to hold him back. The sight of U.S. congressmen (from the same political party, no less) preventing each other from engaging in a physical altercation drew gasps—quite the feat in a chamber that has become all too accustomed to disorder.

Kevin McCarthy had been walking away from Gaetz but spun around amid the commotion. He had just lost the fourteenth consecutive vote in his bid for Speaker—a historic humiliation. Watching the scene play out and presumably calculating that the prospect of a physical brawl on the House floor wouldn't inspire much confidence in his ongoing bid to grasp the gavel, McCarthy took a few steps toward the turmoil before stopping, shoulders slumped, to merely absorb what was unfolding before him as Rogers was shuttled away from the scene.

In an environment where optics are paramount, the implications of a fistfight on the floor of the House of Representatives were not ideal. Even without the scuffle, evocative of overserved Chads in a dive bar, the process had already proven disastrous for the Republicans. They would endure one final round of voting—fifteen in total—before McCarthy finally limped his way onto the dais. It was a Pyrrhic victory for the California lawmaker—the longest Speaker vote since the pre–Civil War era and a mark of shame that foreshadowed an embarrassingly short stint with the gavel.

As the scene unfolded, Matt Gaetz—the target of the fury—remained seated defiantly, the vision of deluded, self-satisfied machismo. Far from appearing disconcerted at the indignity on display, he seemed to revel in the chaos—as if fueled by the hostility and the mayhem. Shortly after the altercation, Gaetz was photographed smiling and pointing to his flexed biceps (which, incidentally, had played no role in the cringeworthy fracas).

This moment in the early days of 2023, however fleeting and forgotten, reflects the state of the modern Republican Party: the dysfunction, the incompetence, the obstinance, the rage, the showmanship, but above all, the utter lack of shame. This is the abject state of a political party that has strayed light-years from its original mission. The professed Party of Lincoln—of Personal Responsibility, of Family Values, of the Constitution itself—was literally at each other's throats as it failed to accomplish the most basic task expected of a governing majority. Today it is controlled by a burgeoning extremist faction for whom compromise is unacceptable and chaos is the goal. The responsibility to govern has been replaced by the need to attack, to perform, to obstruct, to provoke. This reality is getting exponentially worse year after year—and as citizens, we are becoming dangerously numb to it.

For those who argue that such dramatics and dysfunction are inevitable in American politics in the wake of the catastrophic presidency of Donald Trump, look back two years. With virtually the same margin of House seats that Republicans had in 2023,

Nancy Pelosi managed the apparently Herculean feat of winning on the first ballot on January 3, 2021, earning the support of 216 Democrats and surpassing the threshold of 214 needed to become Speaker. The vote was a straightforward task, one that the Democratic majority accomplished handily.

Pelosi took her place on the dais, offering notes of gratitude, hope, and a promise to meet the needs of a country that had been brought to its knees by a pandemic, an economic recession, and an election subversion campaign so aggressive that it would lead to a failed coup attempt by the outgoing Republican president only three days later. "It is my great honor to preside over this sacred ritual of renewal as we gather under the dome of this temple of democracy to begin the 117th Congress," she said, before graciously congratulating Kevin McCarthy. "I look forward to working with you to meet the needs of the American people during this great moment of challenge." Through her enthusiasm, gratitude, and grace—while speaking from behind a mask—she also acknowledged to the new members that "as we are sworn in today, we accept a responsibility as daunting and demanding as any previous generation of leadership has ever faced."

Her speech would portend a historically productive Congress, and serve as a foil to the mayhem that would consume the same chamber a mere two years later. More significantly, it would serve as proof that government works when run by competent people who want it to work.

It also reminds us that, as inescapable as our present death spiral back to Trump appears to be, it's not. We do have an alternative, and a functioning one at that. But there is no denying that our democracy is, once again, teetering on a razor's edge. In such moments, two vital questions present themselves:

How did we get here? And, more urgently, how do we get out?

1

THE ROAD TO SHAMELESSNESS

In July 2023, the Biden administration debuted a thirty-five-second ad featuring a surprisingly effective, if unwitting, spokesperson. She delivered a stirring address, comparing the president's legislative accomplishments to those of two of the most influential, defining, and consequential Democratic presidents of the twentieth century, drawing a direct line from Franklin D. Roosevelt to Lyndon B. Johnson to Joseph R. Biden.

"Joe Biden had the largest public investment in social infrastructure and environmental programs that is actually finishing what FDR started, that LBJ expanded on, and Joe Biden is attempting to complete," she proclaims with conviction.

A montage animates the screen with hero shots of President Biden and Vice President Kamala Harris engaging with everyday Americans. It features heartening images of Biden signing legislation, addressing a Philly union hall, touring a Durham factory, and chopping it up with cops, construction workers, and grateful supporters of all stripes. He looks like the kind of guy you could grab a beer with, the kind of guy who would chase you down half a block to return your wallet, the kind of guy who could deliver on the promise of America.

The ad continues as the female narrator lists the Biden administration's crucial efforts and investments: "Programs to address education, medical care, urban problems, rural poverty, transportation, Medicare, Medicaid, labor unions . . . and he still is working on it."

The music swells. Smash cut to white. Goose bumps.

It was perhaps the most effective messaging yet delivered from the reelection campaign, and every word was accurate. But the ad was especially remarkable because the woman offering such an impressive catalog of Democratic triumphs was Republican congresswoman and top contender for the GOP's most proficient zone-flooder of shit, Marjorie Taylor Greene.

Greene's sound bite was lifted from remarks she'd given earlier that month at an event called the Turning Point Action Conference. She had either been addressing an audience who feels we should get rid of Social Security, Medicare and Medicaid, assisted living facilities, interstate highways, higher education, and a government that serves its citizens; or she was speaking to supporters so conditioned that they will cheer or jeer on cue, without listening to what's being said or evaluating how it might affect their lives. Either way, it made the fact that her rant would serve as a pro-Biden ad all the more poetic.

But before marveling at Greene's characteristic ignorance (don't worry, we'll get to that), and before questioning why the Democrats have yet to deliver as persuasive a message about their own administration's accomplishments, it's worth doing a quick survey of who and what she was attempting to criticize when she invoked these two former presidents.

I am neither a historian nor a political scientist. I don't possess a profound knowledge of the consequences of the two presidents' terms in office. A veritable ocean of ink has been spilled on these subjects, with some of our finest writers and thinkers examining the heritage of our political past to contextualize the present.

The congresswoman from Georgia who has blamed Jewish space lasers for national wildfires . . . is not one of those thinkers.

But Dr. Heather Cox Richardson, who pens the esteemed newsletter *Letters from an American*, is. I spoke with her to get a better grasp of how precedent informs today's tempestuous political climate. FDR's and LBJ's terms did lay the groundwork for some of Biden's greatest successes—even as his administration struggles to draw adequate attention to that reality. Their feats, accomplished during extraordinarily challenging periods, offer hope that Biden's plans could help the country avoid its current risk of plunging headlong into a fascist state.

Greene's head-scratching sentiment and then the ad—using a Republican's emphatic, no-frills speech to inform the public about Democrats' achievements—provoke questions that are within my purview, questions I've been grappling with publicly since 2018. Namely, questions that concern political messaging; the way the GOP has weaponized theirs as a permission structure to behave antithetically to their own professed values; and how they've continued exploiting the same values for decades, even as their language has devolved so radically—from suspect wording to bald-faced lies to openly violent rhetoric.

BUT FIRST LET'S EXPLORE THE HISTORY THAT MARJORIE TAYLOR Greene so blindly wields as a cudgel. What was it that FDR started? Throughout an unusually lengthy tenure, he acted on the conviction that the government was the greatest hope for extracting the United States from the bleak years of the Great Depression. His focus was relatively straightforward: federal intervention, bolstering the working class, expanding the social safety net, and rescuing the economy through financial regulation. His landmark New Deal created Social Security, unemployment benefits, and federal agriculture assistance. Early Republicans, based mainly in the North, had upheld a few morsels of the liberty-oriented, forward-thinking policies on which the party was founded. But such thinking would not prove sustainable for the Grand Old Party. That Republican Party has little to do with today's, beyond their commitment to protecting the wealthy—that element of their DNA has survived. They had plenty of time to strategize while in the minority: Roosevelt's three reelections, the succession of Harry S. Truman to the presidency in 1945, and his narrow win three years later kept the Republicans out of the Oval Office for two decades.*

Fast-forward to the mid-1960s, when it became evident that the Constitution's aim of "We the People" and "a more perfect Union" promised more than many were willing to share. When Greene mockingly speaks of the work that "LBJ expanded on," she (or the aide who handed her the speech in exchange for the AR-15 Greene had presumably been posing with) was referring to Medicare and Medicaid, the pivotal Civil Rights Act of 1964, and the Voting Rights Act of 1965—all of which Johnson passed into law. Lyndon Johnson did not hide his agenda to federally abolish discrimination, and a robust majority of Americans were on board. But not all. With Jim Crow being dismantled before their eyes, a cohort of Republicans shifted course and ignited the "Southern strategy" to gain more political support from white Democrats and

---

* Be still, my heart . . .

lure them to their party. The GOP appealed to segregationists and white supremacists, restructuring the conservative party accordingly. Decades later, the ex-host of *The Celebrity Apprentice* would re-ignite this approach and win over some "very fine people" using similar tactics and guiding principles: racism, fear, and anger.

Nevertheless, what FDR started, what LBJ expanded, and what Biden is still working on is the evolving *idea* of America. If you've listened to a handful of the president's speeches, notably his first reelection campaign speech of January 2024, delivered at Valley Forge, you know how passionate he is about that legacy:

> *We're the only nation in the history of the world built on an idea— not hyperbole—built on an idea: "We hold these truths to be self-evident, that all men and women are created equal."*
>
> *It's an idea declared in the Declaration, created in a way that we viewed everybody as equal and [that they] should be treated equally throughout their lives. We've never fully lived up to that. We have a long way to go. But we've never walked away from the* idea.

Radical Republicans have long been crafting a different kind of idea—not one that would advance America's promise so much as one that has lawmakers seeking (and at times succeeding) to control the levers of power in Washington. Their strategy? As is so often the case, it's pretty simple, at least on the surface:

Oppose. Establish dysfunction. Blame the others.

THE VISIONS OF THE PARTIES WERE NOT ALWAYS SO DISPARATE. IN the aftermath of World War II, Americans were imbued with a sense of optimism and opportunity, of possibility and prosperity. Mind you, it was not an idyllic, naive time: the nation was still recovering from a global war, and well-founded anxiety was brewing over Soviet ambition, Communism in China, and the existential implications of the threat of nuclear war. But politics, besides the fever dream of McCarthyism, was mostly civil, foreign policy bills tended to be broadly bipartisan, and neither party was running campaigns intentionally fueled by brazen bullshit and manipulation schemes . . . just yet. Most Americans were offered a measure of support from the government and its programs.

Of course, plenty of people remained on the margins of society and were denied full access to the American Dream. With the dawn of the lively 1960s, those marginalized groups started asking for an equal slice of apple pie, ushering in the era when the chasm between the two parties became undeniable. Richardson cites President Richard Nixon as "the last traditional Republican trying to hold off, or at least just work with, the movement conservatives—rather than kowtowing to them. In the first two years of the Nixon administration, he seesawed back and forth between these movement conservatives who wanted to go back to the 1920s and the Eisenhower Republicans." Then came the highly polarizing 1970 shooting at Kent State, when the Ohio National Guard fired into a crowd of young student demonstrators protesting the Vietnam War—killing four, wounding nine, and inspiring a nationwide student strike. The shooting also made evident the sharp ideological divide among Americans around the question of patriotism and caused Nixon to lose the confidence of many who had previously supported him. He entered the election of 1972 with a very different kind of attitude, motivation, and strategic plan than when he had first run for president. Several of the methods and strategies he employed from that jaded bag of GOP tools have been wielded in just about every election since, and they remain on display in our current political environment.

The Republican strategy that would ultimately deliver an insurrectionist into power has essentially been a long con, constructed over decades. Mehdi Hasan, the British American journalist, author, and CEO of the media company Zeteo, assisted in tracking it with me. But he cautioned against the word "con," as the GOP's plans have all been laid out, largely in plain sight, ever since the Nixon era.

"On the one hand, it is a con because they're pretending to be the party of populism, the party of family values. *That* is a con. On the other hand, what they're planning to do is out there if you're willing to go find it. They're not hiding the tax cut plans. They're not hiding the racist plans. They're not hiding their intention to tear up democracy, certainly not now, under Trump. But even ten, twenty, thirty years ago, that was the case."

Indeed, the Republicans' top judicial minds wrote down their strategy, primarily in an explicit call to action (complete with detailed instructions) commonly known as the Powell memo.

Lewis F. Powell was a tall, slim, bespectacled attorney with fierce ambition. Senator Sheldon Whitehouse describes him as "a tough and incisive lawyer, willing and able to make sharp, even harsh, decisions . . . well-settled in the White male social and corporate elite of Richmond, VA." A prominent, serious citizen, Powell sat on nearly a dozen major corporate boards, enabling him to observe that antiwar protests and the movements for civil rights and women's rights were disrupting all-white boardrooms and ruffling the feathers of the comfortably elite men who occupied those executive suites.

The DC-based U.S. Chamber of Commerce commissioned Powell to put together a confidential plan for reestablishing corporate authority. His seminal report, "Attack on American Free Enterprise System," opens with an edgy, dramatic declaration: "No thoughtful person can question that the American economic system is under broad attack." It concludes, "Business and the enterprise system are in deep trouble, and the hour is late." The "broad attack" to which Powell was referring—in a tone more apt for warning villagers of bloody warfare against the Vikings—was written in response to threats like public health groups linking tobacco to lung cancer. The [it] audacity!

His memo, which recommended that corporate powers cease all acts of compromise, has since served as a de facto blueprint for the conservative movement. Through the use of fearmongering rhetoric—"frontal assault," "battles," repeated use of the word "attack"—it aimed to persuade corporate leaders that they were engaged in a war for their freedom. Corporations had to cease efforts to compromise, it insisted, as "the ultimate issue may be survival." The Powell memo was extremely specific, detailing a full-on propaganda effort to be funded by businesses' advertising budgets. It dictated that corporations should strategically place speakers on college campuses and monitor textbooks for the potential bias of their content. The dangers of "liberal" and "far left" faculty members were cited repeatedly, establishing them as enemies. Much attention was given to the importance of directing corporate presence and resources to radio broadcasts and TV networks.

Powell emphasized the value of applying pressure to ensure optimal power and influence in the political arena, as well as the necessity of punishing those who opposed such efforts. Though confidential, the report was leaked and eventually published, giving businessmen a method for maintaining power. All it required was persistence and discipline—qualities traditional Republicans proved themselves capable of sustaining.

Finally, the memo explains the necessity of gaining control of the courts and "exploiting judicial action." Powell states that "the judiciary may be the most important instrument for social, economic and political change." And he would reach the top tier to help prove as much. He submitted his report in August 1971. Two months later, President Nixon nominated Powell to the Supreme Court. The following January, he was sworn in as an associate justice. He remained on the highest court in the land for the next fifteen years.

The idea of "positive polarization," a notion pushed especially hard by Pat Buchanan, who served as Nixon's "opposition researcher,"* pissed-off-voter whisperer, and movement conservative speechwriter, came into play at about the same time Powell ascended to the Supreme Court. Richardson confirmed the enthusiasm felt for this idea of winning over voters by pushing divisiveness: "Vice President Spiro Agnew took to it like a duck to water. When Agnew talked about positive polarization, it was positive in the sense that it convinced Republicans to stick with Nixon because those *other* guys were so bad by comparison . . . so Nixon really started that polarization, and then of course Reagan injected it with steroids."

Though today he's burnished as a modern ideal of Republican governance, in reality—behind the smile and the charm he had honed as the host of *General Electric Theater*—Reagan was a leader who succeeded in breaking down more than he built up, and in filling Americans with a sense of distrust in the system. His infamous inaugural statement "Government is not the solution to our problem, government is the problem" was taken to heart by masses of Americans.

A succession of bad-faith politicians seized on the approach of beating opponents by stressing ideological distinctions. If lies

---

* Fancyspeak for those who seek dirt.

were required to achieve that end? Go for it. Energizing coalitions of angry, small-minded white men? Sure. Violence? Naturally. Among the most enduring proponents of the strategy was Newt Gingrich, a military brat elected to Congress in 1979 after two failed bids. Once he secured his seat, he and his perma-smug expression set out to poison the chamber with a new level of dysfunction. He applied himself to breaking the Democrats' control over the House by pitting the parties against each other. He threw wrenches into commonsense legislation, sowed discord, and polluted the political process.

The goal? Make Americans so disgusted with government that they would lose trust in whoever was in power. The Gingrich model may sound familiar; it included "name-calling, conspiracy theories, and strategic obstructionism." All were employed to establish dysfunction as a policy in and of itself. The Democrats were made to appear incapable of getting anything accomplished. Overhyped scandal politics, often of the baseless variety, were another tool frequently used to humiliate opponents.

Richardson offered a theory as to why these chaos architects (Buchanan, Agnew, Gingrich, even Reagan) and those who benefitted from their systems were able to manipulate and experiment with the government: because "they expected that the guardrails would hold. I always think of them like toddlers: toddlers fight against their parents because they know their parents aren't going to throw them in the trash, and they behave well for someone who they think *might* throw them in the trash. They could do all this because they knew they could get away with it, because American democracy was so strong. They were provocateurs deliberately, to put themselves in power. They were all about power." Unfortunately, it paid off. The toddlers continued taking advantage of waves of populism and national anger, while their system of disruptive governance empowered or inspired antagonistic characters beyond the Capitol, like talk radio host Rush Limbaugh.

Gingrich gained power and held sway in the House while behaving just as he had encouraged young Republicans to act before he had even been elected to Congress. He'd advised them to "learn to 'raise hell,' to stop being so 'nice,' to realize that politics was, above all, a cutthroat 'war for power'—and to start acting like it." If only he'd gotten accepted into art school.

He and a dozen fellow aspiring Scout leader types, buoyed by a false sense of self-importance, ceased compromising on bipartisan legislation. C-SPAN was launched in March 1979, and Gingrich's tree-house gang, the Conservative Opportunity Society, would make sure to seek out the cameras. Once handed a mic, they spent an inordinate amount of time demonizing their liberal colleagues and the wider establishment.

University of Maryland political scientist Lilliana Mason identified that Gingrich instructed Republicans to use words such as "betray, bizarre, decay, destroy, devour, greed, lie, pathetic, radical, selfish, shame, sick, steal, and traitors" when speaking about Democrats. Please, Newt, don't hold back.

Gingrich shamelessly cultivated such discourse in front of those C-SPAN cameras and encouraged his colleagues to follow suit. Overblown attacks on Democrats were repeated and aired, assisting in sowing confusion and sparking rage among viewers, and beckoning the media to become an essential vehicle for spewing political garbage.

Later in his career, Gingrich would deflect a question about an extramarital affair he was having: "I think the destructive, vicious, negative nature of much of the news media makes it harder to govern this country, harder to attract decent people to run for public office." The irony of his response is that he is perhaps unilaterally responsible for much of the acrimony in politics and political coverage today. If you're seeking the core contributors to the breakdown of our political discourse, be sure to include Gingrich.

Gingrich and his cronies made huge strides in establishing the policy of dysfunction. Though our forty-fifth president accelerated this policy in an abhorrent, sensationalistic fashion, he was and is merely an extension of the nihilistic, radical politics of decades prior to his emergence as a candidate. The GOP transformation into a pack of needy followers was in place well before he entered the scene.

Other tools helped sharpen the dysfunction, and we'll get to those. The rise of a problematically biased mainstream media ecosystem, finding election loopholes to exploit, preventing young people and minorities from voting, undermining the validity of election results . . . all of these strategies took root early and remain essential to the modern Republican playbook.

Considering the manipulation and resources devoted to stopping our democracy from functioning, it inspires some shred of hope that—big picture—Republicans are *still* coming up short.

THE LONG, ENGINEERED SLIDE OF GOP DYSFUNCTION WAS CREATED with frightening intention and also, to Hasan's earlier point, transparency. Theirs has not been an operation executed in invisible ink or behind closed doors. It's never been a hidden venture, Hasan argues, "whether on the judicial and the corporate front with the Powell memo, or the media front." The latter is referring to Roger

Ailes's idea, described in a memo prior to Nixon's impeachment, "A Plan for Putting the GOP on TV News," to set up a network very much like what Fox "News" became just over twenty years later. Australian billionaire Rupert Murdoch supported the effort and launched the cable network in 1996, enabling the right to rebrand the Democrats with messaging that made its way into millions of homes.

Twenty-one months preceding Fox's debut was the first Republican majority in the House in four decades. Republican strategy thrived and populism exploded, as Americans were conned into believing that the party represented traditional values and a promise of prosperity.

A decade later, along came the uncompromising, self-proclaimed Young Guns: Eric Cantor, Kevin McCarthy, and Paul Ryan. They took several chapters out of Gingrich's ragebook and ran with them, traveling around the country fueling anger at the political establishment in 2009. They recruited radicals, exploited the desperate anger felt after the financial collapse and the backlash against Obama, and promised to blow up the establishment in Washington. They hoped to use that frustration to catapult themselves into the majority. They delegitimized the government. They and other colleagues made governing norms seem optional.

These guys were never the directors of the performances we're seeing today, but they were fantastic stagehands and roadies for propping them up. They operated under the monumentally stupid assumption that radicals and the Tea Party movement would fall in line and . . . then what? Celebrate their rise to power and become putty in their hands? Not so much. Instead, each of the Guns would be chewed up and spit out by the forces they had helped nurture. Cantor would lose his seat to a Tea Party radical; Ryan would basically be forced to leave by the fresh radical right; and in 2023 McCarthy would resign after being dethroned by similar forces in an even more spectacular and mortifying manner.

Upon exiting, that last remaining Gun spoke about his colleagues' untrustworthiness and motivation. "I'm not quite sure those individuals are looking to be productive," said McCarthy. "It concerns me as a Republican based upon watching what they do. I want to be a Republican and a conservative that governs. And we're going to have to find our way to do that." Funny how buttressing the Republican ranks with clowns and extremists was never an issue for Kevin McCarthy until the very moment that it became personally inconvenient for him.

By 2010, shortly after the activity of the Tea Party movement had crested, Republicans introduced Project REDMAP, the goal of which was to win control of state legislatures ahead of redistricting in a successful effort to gerrymander both legislative and congressional maps. As elections lawyer Marc Elias, the national authority on voting rights, explained, "Project REDMAP was one of the first concerted efforts to weaponize redistricting. Gerrymandering really has two eras. Those who say there's always been gerrymandering are correct. But states were initially gerrymandered to protect incumbents or more parochial state interests—it was not based on party. Also, they didn't have technological capabilities to gerrymander in the way in which we currently think about it. People would look at paper maps and identify what might be good areas for them or their candidate. What Project REDMAP did was it came at the perfect period, when computer technology had evolved to allow gerrymandering to be done with a lot more precision. And it was right after the Tea Party movement. So there was a convergence of two things: a hyper-partisan impulse on the side of the Republicans, and new technology to execute it. But it was always an effort to weaponize the redistricting process and ruthlessly engage in partisan gerrymandering." It was, of course, highly intentional and strategic.

"The Republicans did not spend tens of millions of dollars developing REDMAP because it didn't matter," Elias noted. "They knew it mattered because they have the same data and analytics around voting that they have around redistricting."

Even with all the far right's tricks and manipulations, however, they couldn't get rid of Obama; nor could they deliver on guarantees to dismantle the status quo in Washington in favor of a more conservative government. They proved themselves capable of finding and enraging constituents—but to what end? Despite vast amounts of money pumped into Republican campaigns, unmet promises left leagues of angry voters feeling let down by *both* sides, unheard and unseen, and consequently distrustful of the government.

Much of America was eager for an outsider candidate. Which is partly why, abetted by no shortage of media hosts, vociferous podcasters, and conspiracy-minded bloggers, Donald J. Trump bumbled in and amplified the notion that both parties had betrayed the American public. His campaign was fueled by the idea that the nation needed a savior from outside the political machine, somebody unaffiliated and thereby able to act on behalf of real people.

Donald Trump for president? Such a ridiculous prospect was (too) quickly written off by those among us who couldn't accept that his bombast would be taken seriously. By the time he *was* taken seriously, he had already released the flames of pent-up anger nationwide, while putting himself forward as the salve. With crucial help from a baffled media that couldn't keep the cameras away from him, he directed that energy toward supporting his candidacy.

Despite his devastating, revealing behavior during his first campaign, which included mocking a disabled reporter, bragging of sexual harassment, slinging racist remarks at will—we all know the list of shame—he still got a larger share of the GOP vote than John McCain or Mitt Romney did in prior campaigns. Did he respond with honor, patriotism, and human decency and eventually curb his repellent behavior or show a modicum of respect for the country?

Of course not. Trump's crude antics were working, so he only raised the volume and attracted more attention to his destructive mission. His ego may as well have been his campaign manager and top advisor, and he merely allowed the sentiment that government was corrupt and unworthy to simmer until it reached a boiling point. As both parties had been made to look weak and ineffectual, this political novice descended from his golden escalator and was ushered into the Oval Office. His (at best) loose affiliation with or interest in the party never seemed to matter. Republicans in Washington accepted Trump as their leader, which yielded high levels of tension within government that he did nothing to extinguish. Republicans who condemned his leadership soon found themselves out of office.

Since Trump's 2016 run and presidency, a few morally sound Republicans have been willing to publicly reject his behavior. They have done so either on their way out or at their own political and personal peril. Liz Cheney, Adam Kinzinger, Ben Sasse, Mitt Romney, and even Mike Pence have, at key moments, stood their ground against Trump and proved they were willing to prioritize their oath of office or vote with the Democrats. I do not mention them to lionize the small sample of Republicans who have behaved with decency. But there are members of the GOP who have resisted being sucked into Trump's deranged vortex. Their longevity in government and their standing within their own party have suffered for it, and those who are still in Washington have allowed themselves to become impotent and irrelevant.

There have been a great many missteps Democrats have made over the years, and weaknesses remain within the party, its methods, and its vehicles for communicating its messaging (or lack thereof). Politicians are human, politics is nothing if not complicated, and there has never been a perfect party. But the intentional dysfunction of the modern Republican Party is an order of magnitude more active and strategic. The perverseness is so extreme that dysfunction redounds to their benefit. As the GOP's ultimate goal is to shrink the size of government by convincing everyone that government can't work, they continue doing their best to break it (for example, voting constantly against funding bills to keep it functioning), and then point to the dysfunction as evidence that government can't work. Of course, what they fail to mention is the reason it can't work is because Republicans intentionally sabotage it. When you have people in power who don't believe in government, that government won't function properly. In *any* organization, when the people in charge are hell-bent on breaking something, it tends to break. The dysfunction isn't some unfortunate by-product; it's the end goal.

Which is why today we see a fractured Republican Party that has lost its identity, its integrity, and—arguably—its collective mind. Radical lawmakers, hungry for the public lens, have relinquished any ideals once held by the GOP. Their center of gravity is an aggressively racist, misogynist, anti-everything narcissist who has a profound admiration for dictators and yearns to be one himself.

Richardson, well-versed in the whens and hows of social change, underscores how dramatically the Republican Party changed from 2015, when Trump first arrived on the scene.

"What Trump did is he took what was an ideological position and turned it into a movement. It's a very different thing now than it was then. The current Republicans are not traditional Republicans, they're this radical right movement that took over the party. What they did is to offer a narrative, a story that made people feel important, at the same time as Democrats and traditional Republicans backed away from stories and instead worked on nailing together coalitions."

The unruly clique of useless so-called politicians who appear to be controlling the GOP today and are so proudly unwilling to get anything done have no recognizable ideals or ambition to better the country. Given that they are desperate for nothing so much as the appearance of power, of course they pose a genuine threat to democracy, something for which they show no regard. But this faction of media fiends—Marjorie Taylor Greene, Jim Jordan, Matt Gaetz, Lauren Boebert, James Comer, Elise Stefanik, and others—are but bleating lambs. Though the stain of their dishonor will remain, they are mere figurines, soon to be forgotten. They are, however, representative of the legitimately dangerous, ideologically radicalized following of our twice-impeached, four-times-indicted former president.

Trump, his name splashed across the tabloids, succeeded in reaching the deep pockets of Americans who felt animosity toward marginalized groups in the country. He embraced the haters and got gobs of press. That drew higher numbers of gun-toting fame seekers to run for office on similar platforms. Those who made it into office have tended to ignore the trivial business of governing, instead focusing on attracting sound bites and building social media followings to bolster their brands. They looked to their filter-free leader and saw the power in sowing chaos. It didn't hurt that, rather than put up resistance to policies like an immediate ban on Muslims, the older and more established members of the government, like then Senate majority leader Mitch McConnell, fell in line immediately with full-throated support.

Of course, it all came to a head in 2021, when Trump, whom the Republicans—let us truly never forget—continue to support breathlessly and near unanimously, made the conscious decision that his last act in office would be to overturn a free and fair election and undermine the Constitution.

If you were to create a mortal enemy of traditional GOP values in a lab, out would emerge Donald Trump himself.

And *still*, we are watching in real time as party members prove—despite the optics, the outspoken hatred, the criminal charges, the high-octane derangement—that they are willing to follow him off a cliff. It's gone far beyond chaos.

The abominable nature of these characters is not a revelation. But so long as Republicans keep elevating clowns to power, they should continue being held to account. Every new voter, every moderate voter, every independent voter who may be wavering about whether to cast a ballot for Republicans should know exactly who they are empowering. It is not the elusive moderates. It is the Marjorie Taylor Greenes and Mike Johnsons: the incompetent, attention-seeking, Christofascist creeps who believe that their job is to impose laws on us that Americans have roundly rejected. These people are not in government to make your lives better, or to lower costs, or to expand health care, or to raise your salary. They're there to tighten their grip on power and insulate themselves from personal accountability—to "Make America Great Again."

Those who are unwavering in their MAGA-support are likely not reading this. But I know there are reasonable Americans who support the GOP and also recognize that the players who are being embraced by today's Republican Party are unacceptable humans, let alone representatives. Tragically, those extremists are the ones being bolstered by every Republican vote—or every non-vote, for that matter.

The GOP that—even at its most deeply conservative moments—accepted the rule of law, the norms of liberal democracy, and the legitimacy of the opposing party? Gone. The party that was once invested in governing, in compromising and negotiating, in having reasonable debates, and in embracing America's responsibility to uphold global order? Gone. The party whose leadership sought to address real needs and problems while resisting conspiracy theories, demagoguery, and temptations toward political violence? Gone.

In place of what was once a civil body, we have a party that prefers temper tantrums to legislation. It appeals to voters by peddling fantasies about stolen elections, while promising to slash government funding, which they claim offers too much to less-deserving Americans: immigrants, women, LGBTQ+ people. Cooperation has become synonymous with treason; bipartisan agreements are trumpeted as the "deep state" in action. The performative, exceptionally well-funded radical right's goal is essentially to lie in the road and make themselves obstacles to a functioning democracy.

We've seen the consequences of electing a leader as stringently shameless as Donald Trump. His moral compass is not broken; it simply doesn't exist. You'd be hard-pressed to find a man who speaks or behaves in a manner that is more bluntly antithetical to every one of the GOP's purported principles. Yet he connects with his audience (and their sense of aggrievement).

Discussing his assets in 2024, Trump acknowledged, "I became president because of the brand." He didn't stop there; he proposed that his name was probably worth $10 billion and was—in his modest estimation—the hottest brand in the world.[*]

LET US NOT FORGET MARJORIE TAYLOR GREENE'S CLOSING WORDS[†] IN the July 2023 Biden ad, "and he is still working on it." Richardson contends that Biden has indeed been a transformational president. "He took office with the idea of rolling back the country . . . that's the idea that he is defending. He is making sure that the government does the four things of the liberal consensus: regulates business, provides a basic social safety net, promotes infrastructure, and protects civil rights." Those support systems were all in place until Reagan came in and started gutting everything. Biden "is deliberately saying," Richardson continues, "'We invest in the American people, *this will work*, and we know it will work because it worked in the 1930s and 1940s and 1950s and 1960s and 1970s.'"

Still, try as we might (and I really, really have), we cannot ignore Biden's opponent. This man, despite having zero political expertise but a lifetime of experience in marketing his own name, remains the center of gravity for the party of unfulfilled promises and punchy slogans. It's fitting, really. So let's examine the right's

---

[*] Although it became $455 million *less* hot after the judgment against him in the New York attorney general's business fraud lawsuit.

[†] Not a phrase I ever thought I would write.

proclaimed ideals, which have been their baseline for decades, and gauge to what extent the party *has* fulfilled its promises. As far as I can tell, if there's any political gulf more extreme than the one between the two parties, it is the abyss between what Republicans say and what they do.

2

LABELS AND LIES

"When anyone calls me a liberal, I say, 'You're damn right,' because at the heart of that word is 'liberty,'" explained law professor, constitutional scholar, and U.S. Congressman Jamie Raskin. "And I'm a progressive, because at the heart of that word is 'progress.' And these days, I'm very happy to call myself a conservative, because unlike the party of nihilists and insurrectionists, I want to conserve the land, air, water, the climate system, the Constitution, the Bill of Rights, the Clean Air Act, the Social Security Act, the Medicare Act, the Fair Labor Standards Act, Civil Rights Act, Voting Rights Act, you name it. Everything they want to tear down is everything we want to conserve and make work for the American people over the decades of progress we've made."

Republicans, by contrast, have spent decades hiding behind their historical branding to give themselves cover to act in a way that is completely antithetical to their professed values. These are conservatives who don't intend to conserve anything; constitutionalists who don't adhere to the Constitution; textualists who are content to discard any text that doesn't confirm their prior beliefs. The Republicans don't even believe in their namesake of a "republic" anymore.

So what *do* they stand for?

Whether you refer to it as branding or spin, talking points or just plain bullshit, if you are engaged in politics, you will endure a daily onslaught of lies. And while no one party has a monopoly on absolute accuracy, only one has cultivated their brand with the express intention of creating an alternate reality. Tiresome though it may be, it is essential to debunk, expose, or at least question radical Republican distortions of the truth, lest they settle and harden as any American's version of reality.

Since I began my work in political media, I've been fortunate enough to learn a great deal from the politicians and political analysts who have shared their views with me and helped inform mine. On the flip side, I've also had to endure a truly overwhelming amount of garbage from radical Republicans. Rebutting their shameless lies, switchbacks, and hypocrisy has become a full-time job. At the beginning, I honestly remember wondering, *What if there's not enough news to keep me busy?* Now I wonder whether I'll ever get enough sleep.

But the occupation of extinguishing GOP lies has become far more challenging—because at the helm of their twisted disinformation mechanism is the walking nightmare that is Donald Trump. In 2020, when Trump first debated Biden, he went on a two-minute rant and lied *every nine seconds*.[*] Chris Wallace made a few paltry attempts to halt the then sitting president's incoherent tirade, but not even the greatest moderator on earth[†] could refute that many lies in real time.

---

[*] As Mehdi Hasan notes in *Win Every Argument* (New York: Henry Holt, 2023).

[†] Jim Downey, the esteemed moderator in the academic decathlon depicted in *Billy Madison*, responds to Billy much as I would have been inclined to respond to Trump: "What you just said is one of the most insanely idiotic things I have ever heard. At no point in your rambling, incoherent response were you even close to anything that could be considered a rational thought. Everyone in this room is now dumber for having listened to it. I award you no points, and may God have mercy on your soul."

Republicans, not unlike sheep, have very strong flocking instincts. They will follow one another—regardless of message— into pastures well outside their comfort zone. Trump or no Trump, Republican politicians and their supporters remain bound together by a convenient bag of branding tricks and talking points. For decades, they have put forward specific "values" as justification for their positions. The more I listened, the more I heard the same phrases repeated.

"Family values; fiscal responsibility; states' rights; pro–law enforcement; upholders of the Constitution." These handy benchmark slogans are still being touted by even the most immoral and hypocritical members of the party.

So how were their so-called values reached in the first place? And how did our modern fringe group of look-at-me Republicans miss the memo regarding the meaning behind the ideals they claim to uphold? Let's take a look . . .

FAMILY VALUES

The volatile, consequential 1960s and 1970s are often cited as the years during which the modern GOP became animated behind the notion that they're the party of traditional Family Values™. It was always a front, used to garner power and make themselves appear safe and sound at a time when the Republican Party was flailing. The defeat in Vietnam, the Watergate scandal, Nixon's resignation, and a wobbly economy left the overwhelmingly white, Christian party in need of a rallying cry. That party viewed itself as being attacked on all sides by those seeking equality (operating under the absurd notion that others' gaining rights is somehow an affront to their own). Racial integration in schools, the Supreme Court's 1973 ruling in *Roe v. Wade*,* and increased awareness of LGBTQ+ rights provoked conservative Republicans to break out their megaphones and shout from some supposed moral high ground. "Family values" proved a crucial shield and sword during this revolutionary era. It would quickly become an essential courting phrase for evangelicals across the country.

The battle against progressive movements was spearheaded by Phyllis Schlafly and other arch-conservatives hoping to convince the public that equality between men and women was undesirable. A powerful activist, Schlafly was known for leading the campaign to prevent ratification of the Equal Rights Amendment, and was one of the first to tap into the power of using "family values" as a partisan divide. Unsanitary issues like abortion rights and equity, she argued, were a massive threat to the sanctity of a strong family.

Simultaneously, Christian schools were revolting against progress being made toward, among other things, racial integration, claiming that such movements endangered—you guessed it—family values. The slogan was appropriated across the party, and "family values" became a cloaked phrase used to oppose anybody seen as "other": immigrants, LGBTQ+ people, women seeking control over their own livelihood.

The GOP has held fast to this very convenient brand as a means of rejecting progressive measures. They still thunder about their party acting as the sole arbiters of a "traditional" American homelife, and continue to offer themselves that moral positioning and permission to impose their agenda on, well, the rest of us.

---

* Confirming that the Constitution protects a woman's right to reproductive autonomy and choice over her own fate . . . imagine that.

Which, in the era of near-uniform fealty to Donald Trump, is especially rich. The same party that has been beating its chest about core family values for decades has sold its collective soul for an alleged criminal with revolting behavior and a more than questionable track record when it comes to family, tradition, and anything that could be construed as morality. And they were prepared to do so before he was even elected.

As everyone remembers, in 2016, one month prior to the November election, the now-infamous *Access Hollywood* tape was published by the *Washington Post*, featuring then candidate Trump explaining the ways in which one's celebrity status can be capitalized on to sexually assault women. Really charming stuff. What's more, his supporters from the party of pure, wholesome values leaped to back him up when he defended his comments as "locker room talk"—you know, the kind that well-heeled family men regularly engage in.

Despite his protestations, this wasn't just talk. Trump has been accused of harassment, sexual abuse, sexual assault, or rape by at least twenty-six women since the 1970s. One of those women, E. Jean Carroll, took Trump to court and won a $5 million civil lawsuit in New York. In a separate defamation case, Judge Lewis A. Kaplan elucidated that Carroll's claim that Trump "did 'rape'" her was "substantially true." After losing—a fate he has proven he cannot handle in any arena, under any circumstances—Trump defamed her again, was taken to court again, and lost again, this time to the tune of $83.3 million. And yet his cult of supporters has chosen to overlook his sins, for which he has shown the opposite of remorse. They have opted instead to cast Trump as the victim while crucifying the actual survivor.

Not to dwell on the reality that this Republican presidential candidate is more skilled at identifying a child's sketch of an elephant* than he is at exhibiting family values . . . but his supporters were also happy to ignore the fact that Trump's former "fixer" Michael Cohen had written checks to buy the silence of Stormy Daniels.† Daniels (whose real name is Stephanie Clifford) is a porn star with whom Donald allegedly had an affair in July 2006—four months after his third wife, Melania, gave birth to their son, Barron. Perhaps there are enough members of their party who are happy to accept this grotesque revision of family values. More likely it highlights just how little the party *actually* cares about its most reiterated slogan, and how willing the GOP is (both inside the Capitol and among the base at large) to excuse Trump for violating everything it claims to stand for. I'm not sure how else to explain why the party of wholesome family values has responded to the behavior of this ambassador of immorality not just with silence . . . but with high-octane rallies.

The fish rots from the head. And an abandonment of family values helped define Trump's presidency, right down to his sad troop of foot soldiers. In 2018, an alarming majority of Republicans supported a bill that forcibly separated undocumented migrant children from their parents as soon as they crossed the southern border. There were devastating consequences for thousands of families, resulting in unspeakable trauma for all those ripped away from mothers, fathers, children. While Democrats protested in horror, U.S. Attorney General Jeff Sessions shamelessly admitted

---

* Which is not to diminish Trump's crowning achievement of passing a test intended to detect dementia . . .

† On the off chance you might doubt the validity of Cohen's claim, he went to prison for his contribution to the torrid affair, among other crimes.

that the policy was meant as a deterrent. Other countries, he said, would "get the message."

Safe to presume that the message he hoped immigrants would "get" was *not* "'Give me your tired, your poor, / Your huddled masses yearning to breathe free . . .'"

Tragically, this inhumane "zero-tolerance" stance flared up again in 2023 and 2024, with Republican candidates teasing the potential of reinstating similar brutality in an effort to outflank each other from the right.

Also worth noting is how limited and specific the party's definition of family is. Since the Schlafly era, it has referred to white, Christian, well-off, heterosexual nuclear families. The Republican Party Platform has stated for decades that "Republicans oppose and resist the efforts of the Democrat Party to redefine the traditional American family." Mike Johnson, Speaker of the House and a fervent Trump hanger-on and election denier, has opposed and resisted this as well, calling homosexuality a "dangerous lifestyle," and writing that legalizing gay marriage would lead to pedophilia and to people marrying their pets, and could potentially destroy "the entire democratic system." Since taking up the gavel and coming under fire for these published statements, he has suggested that he loves the Bible and the rule of law and doesn't remember writing the things he wrote, not unlike the way George Santos conveniently couldn't quite recall using campaign funds for Botox and Ferragamo sneakers.

His extremist colleagues, peddling their "Don't Say Gay" laws, are delighted to have the most powerful Republican in the House voicing their bigoted opinions. "This is a free country, but we don't give special protections for every person's bizarre choices,"

Johnson wrote. He's one to talk about bizarre choices. This proud evangelical Christian uses his son as his "accountability partner" so that they can track each other's pornography usage.* Just like Jesus would've wanted?

Sexual assault, paternal negligence, policies that tear apart families, disrespect for a non-heteronormative family structure. How has not a single one of these proven to be a red flag or even an apparent subject of grave concern to a party that claims to not just abide by, but *be the sole proponent of*, family values? Perhaps Republicans are deluded enough to believe that their party continues to excel at protecting the sanctity of the home. Either that or the phrase serves as a threadbare veil of moral superiority; as language used to dictate how all Americans should live their lives—in their choice of partner, in what they read, in how they pray; on abortion, even in cases of rape . . . hypothetically committed by the type of man who would brag about grabbing women by the pussy.

MEANWHILE, DEMOCRATS ARE TAKING MEASURES TO PROTECT families and to ensure that they're supported. In late 2022, President Biden signed the Respect for Marriage Act, which codified marriage equality for same-sex couples and interracial couples into federal law. The law protects already married couples and ensures that families are not separated; 169 House Republicans and 36 Senate Republicans voted against it. After all, why would the Party of Family Values want to preserve . . . families?

President Biden also signed the Violence Against Women

---

* Yes, this is real. No, I am not exaggerating.

Reauthorization Act, expanding the legislation to increase funding to states and territories to better support "survivors of domestic violence, dating violence, sexual assault, and stalking." Naturally, 172 Republicans voted against it. Nothing should surprise me anymore . . . but it's still striking to imagine *opposing* legislation called the Violence Against Women Act.

Surely—*surely*—they'll stand up for children, though?

Nope, not interested in helping them either. The Party of Family Values has attempted to loosen child labor laws, eliminate life-saving health care for transgender and nonbinary kids, and make it a priority to ban free school lunches. Every MAGA Republican in Congress voted against expanding the child tax credit. Republicans consistently vote against childcare. They vote against universal pre-K. They vote against SNAP (food stamps), even though nearly half of SNAP recipients are for families with children. They vote against Medicaid, when, *again*, around half of the non-elderly recipients are children under the age of nineteen. When Republicans stripped women of their reproductive rights, young girls were forced to give birth after being assaulted. I think it's fair to say that on no planet in this solar system could any of that be viewed as beneficial to American children.

Interrogated about his senseless stance against the child tax credit, GOP Senator John Thune justified his No vote by stating that he wasn't getting "good vibes" on striking a deal with Democrats. But this time, there was no way of hiding behind family values to explain away his coarse vote. When prodded to detail why he would actively reduce the quality of life for a majority of American families in need, he reached into his party's trusted branding sack and pulled out a convenient excuse, despite its having an equally dubious basis in fact.* House Republicans claimed they sought such extreme cuts for essential programs for mothers and children due to the importance of upholding "fiscal responsibility."

FISCAL RESPONSIBILITY

Remember: the *kids* spend recklessly while the *parents* have to pay the bills. That's how Republicans like to present the relationship, as long as they're cast as the parents, of course: the reasonable ones with the bank accounts and knowhow, grinning condescendingly beneath their party's banner of "fiscal responsibility."†

For most of modern history, Republicans have prided themselves on being superior when it comes to financial matters: they're the side that adheres to low government spending and tax cuts, all the while promising economic growth and bulging pockets. But that just hasn't been the case. Not for a very long time. Though the GOP rests comfortably under this false advertisement, the notion of their party as being more fiscally responsible is a farce.

Ronald Reagan played a significant role in launching this deceit, booming it out as a major talking point throughout his campaign. During stump speeches, he regularly told the story of a supposed "welfare queen" from Chicago who drove a Cadillac and was living large, having ripped off the government and everybody's tax money.

---

* Fact (noun): an antiquated notion that once mattered.

† Notwithstanding the plain record of ballooning deficits and consistent economic calamity.

The imagery stuck with people, and was exploited when he was pushing cuts to programs that helped the poor. He became president, grinned for the cameras, and nearly tripled our national debt. The three Republican presidents we've had since have each only added to the debt—though somehow the Democrats are always to blame for leading the nation into financial despair.

From 2017 to 2019, the Republicans gained full control of government. There was to be no pointing fingers across the aisle at the Democrats, who for the moment had been relegated to the minority and couldn't exercise any discernible degree of power. *Surely* this would have been a prime opportunity for the GOP to take an ax to the deficit. After all, that's exactly what then candidate Trump cavalierly promised in March 2016: in an interview with Bob Woodward, he said that he would "get rid of the $19 trillion in debt." Woodward asked how long that would take:

DT: *I think I could do it fairly quickly, because of the fact the numbers—*

BW: *What's fairly quickly?*

DT: *Well, I would say over a period of eight years. And I'll tell you why*

BW: *Would you ever be open to tax increases as part of that, to solve the problem?*

DT: *I don't think I'll need to. The power is trade. Our deals are so bad.*

Trump did not "get rid of" the debt. The 2017 tax cut, which the Congressional Budget Office (CBO) estimated would *add* $1.9 trillion to the federal deficit over a decade, was passed by 95 percent of House Republicans and 100 percent of Senate Republicans before being signed into law by Trump. That tax cut included slashing the corporate tax rate from 35 percent to 21 percent, which effectively dried up federal revenues, thereby increasing the deficit. And Trump's silver bullet of overcoming it via trade deals? Oh, what he meant—by all appearances—was that he intended to launch a global trade war. Which you won't be surprised to learn also didn't exactly do wonders for the deficit.

That ambitious, bragged-over plan to eliminate $19 trillion in debt? Not quite. By the time his term was over, he and congressional Republicans had increased the national debt by $7.8 trillion. It was the third-biggest increase of any U.S. presidential administration, despite not paying off a war.[*]

This wasn't purely financial mismanagement. The Republicans maneuvered this precisely as intended; they just didn't frame it that way. You've got to hand it to them: they had a clear goal, and they achieved it. The problem, for anybody with a conscience, is that their goal was to help the wealthiest Americans (particularly those inclined to donate to their campaigns) conveniently get wealthier.

For all the debate that goes into comprehending why many of the wealthiest American voters, even those who appear to be reasonable, continue to vote for the Republican ticket—no matter its face, and regardless of whether that face has been featured on a recent mug shot—it's often the case that you don't have to look much deeper than the contents of said voters' wallets. For the first

---

* And no, the War on Christmas doesn't count.

time in history, the wealthiest Americans paid a lower effective tax rate than the bottom 50 percent of Americans by 2018. The only way this could've been more of a gift to those wealthiest Americans was if it had come with a first-class ticket to Davos.

In his first formal press conference as Speaker, Mike Johnson, considered a *true conservative* by the radical right, promised "a return to 'fiscal responsibility.'" Shortly after, he introduced his first major bill—a $14 billion emergency aid package for Israel with an equal "offset" in the form of reduced funding for the IRS, which had been allocated as part of Biden's Inflation Reduction Act to catch wealthy tax cheats. One tiny problem: the "offset" wouldn't offset anything so much as it would *add* to the deficit.* Johnson's bill made it evident that deficit reduction was not his priority. It was merely a front for using political capital to immediately serve the ultrawealthy—and not just the ultrawealthy. The IRS was clear about its target: those with incomes exceeding $1 million . . . who owed more than $250,000 in outstanding tax debt. In other words, the Republicans sought to bail out not only preposterously wealthy Americans but preposterously wealthy Americans who were also tax cheats.

Frankly, there is no fiscal floor when it comes to what the GOP will seek to destroy in pursuit of political gain, which was put on stark display in the summer of 2023. The United States would have defaulted if the debt ceiling wasn't raised by June 5, according to the Treasury Secretary. The debt ceiling needed to be raised to allow the government to meet its existing finan-

---

* The IRS commissioner projected that the bill would add as much as $90 billion to the deficit over the subsequent decade. A more conservative estimate by the nonpartisan CBO estimated that it would result in nearly $27 billion in lost revenue.

cial obligations—that is, to pay the bill for what's already been spent. This process had played out without fail seventy-eight times since the 1960s, but by the last week of May 2023, the Republican-led House still hadn't raised the debt ceiling, opting instead to hold the economy hostage in exchange for political concessions from the Democrats, which included stripping away most of the very popular Inflation Reduction Act and imposing work requirements on social programs—precisely the type of agenda that would only succeed by way of this kind of under-handed maneuvering.

If the U.S. defaulted on its debt, the results would be cat-astrophic. Basic functions of the federal government would cease, the U.S.'s credit rating would get downgraded, financial markets—both domestic and international—would crater, the dollar would risk its spot as the world's reserve currency, interest rates would rise on a raft of loans, the capital market would freeze, and we would likely fall into a recession. As my friends at *Pod Save America* like to say: "Not great, Dan."

MEANWHILE, THE DEMOCRATS ARE TAKING STEPS TO IMPROVE our nation's finances. The Inflation Reduction Act invested in IRS efforts aimed at clawing back unpaid taxes from tax-dodging corporations and high-income earners, a constituency for whom enforcement plummeted during the Trump presidency. This came on the heels of the American Rescue Plan, which saved the U.S. economy after COVID and launched the fastest recovery of all G7 countries. Which is to say nothing of Biden presiding over the addition of more than 15 million jobs (including 800,000 manu-facturing jobs), rising wages, falling inflation, a record high stock market, the creation of the greatest number of small businesses in

U.S. history, and the longest stretch of sub–4 percent unemployment in over half a century.

Ultimately, while Republicans have been consistent in claiming that they're fiscally responsible, behavior like cushioning the blow for ultrawealthy tax cheats or flirting with defaulting on the debt and risking a recession is anything but responsible.

STATES' RIGHTS

During the era of "what LBJ expanded on," namely pushing through the triumphant Civil Rights Act, figures like Senator Barry Goldwater beckoned voters to the GOP by explicitly campaigning on "states' rights," long understood to be a veiled call for anti-Black voters, given its history as a justification for slavery. It proved a valuable turn of phrase during the presidential campaigns of Richard Nixon, Ronald Reagan, and Donald Trump—all of whom found a strong crop of voters by appealing to estranged or disillusioned whites who didn't trust the federal government or any progressive legislation. Courting racists has been central to Republican strategy well before Trump urged the Proud Boys, a neo-fascist militant organization, to "stand back and stand by."

The GOP has continued championing the catchphrase to limit government interference, often to ensure a measure of segregation, or—with modern-day Republicans—as a cowardly means of getting their way in defiance of the federal government.

In 2020, Texas attorney general Ken Paxton filed the lawsuit *Texas v. Pennsylvania* with the United States Supreme Court, contesting the election results in four other states that Joe Biden had won: Georgia, Michigan, Pennsylvania, and Wisconsin. The day after Paxton filed the suit, 18 Republican attorneys general, 126 Republican lawmakers, and Donald Trump signed on to the effort. Because nothing promotes an understanding of or a respect for states' rights quite like one state taking it upon itself to try to undo election results in four other states.

The danger and folly of this scheme was so obvious that even a few Republicans criticized it. Texas Congressman Chip Roy tweeted, "I believe the case itself represents a dangerous violation of federalism & sets a precedent to have one state asking federal courts to police the voting procedures of other states." Texas Senator John Cornyn said, "I frankly struggle to understand the legal theory" behind it.

It *would* have set a dangerous precedent, and there was *no* valid legal theory behind it, which is why even the current 6–3 conservative U.S. Supreme Court declined to hear the case. When you're outflanking Clarence Thomas and Samuel Alito on the right, you may have fallen off the edge.

More recently, the caustic issue of abortion has placed Republicans' shameless disregard for states' autonomy on full display. For half a century, the GOP had been trying to overturn *Roe v. Wade*, all the while claiming that the right to an abortion should be decided by the states. On June 24, 2022, the decision in *Dobbs v. Jackson Women's Health Organization* overturned *Roe*. Were Republicans satisfied with the issue being decided at the state level, as the right had long been proposing? Of course not. It took all of eleven weeks before consistently inconsistent Senator Lindsey Graham and Representative Chris Smith introduced nationwide abortion ban bills in the Senate and House. In fewer than three months they had dropped all pretense of wanting abortion to be a state issue.

In November 2023, just days after voters opted to enshrine those rights in the Ohio state constitution, four Republican lawmakers in that state set out to strip judges of their power to interpret the new abortion rights amendment because they didn't like the outcome. Consequently, they went on a mission to undo the referendum that voters had just passed. The state had spoken. Its very conservative base had made it clear that they didn't want the government to control their bodies. Nevertheless, the four Republicans responded in true Trumpian fashion, by sidestepping and disregarding the will of voters.

As Marc Elias confirmed, "Of course that's not legal. They've been attempting multiple avenues of illegality to try to prevent this initiative from going into effect. They've claimed that there was ambiguity in the language as to what this referendum does." (A laughably inaccurate suggestion—before the vote, they had boasted of how explicit the wording was.)

"The language is very clear, and the Republicans know it," Elias said, "and they knew it was clear when they were trying to mess around to keep it from going into effect."

In all, it amounts to another example from a party that does not respect the rule of law. They lost a referendum fair and square, so they immediately tried to figure out one way or another to undermine it. It is disingenuous, it's lawless, and it's antidemocratic.

When elected officials* extravagantly refuse to abide by the edicts of our most crucial and distinguished institutions, it's hardly a wonder that their constituents get the message: if you

---

* For small-bit examples from other small minds, see Governors Greg Abbott pushing for buoy borders, Kay Ivey of Alabama fighting redistricting, and Ron DeSantis fighting for the death penalty . . . each of them in defiance of either the Supreme Court or the Department of Justice.

don't get your way, storm the gates, smash through the windows of the Capitol, and—for good measure—smear shit all over it like petulant truants. And should you run into law enforcement along the way, don't hesitate to use those flagpoles of yours as bludgeons.

PRO—LAW ENFORCEMENT

Republicans have traditionally supported a strong, heavily armed national defense and domestic wall of aggression. Reagan massively increased expenditure on U.S. military forces. From there, being pro-military stuck as part of their brand. It's an allegiance they continue to boast of, as is their way, even as their actions have communicated a far different reality.

Alabama Senator Tommy Tuberville held up 452 Pentagon nominations for nearly the whole of 2023 to protest a Department of Defense policy that reimburses costs for military members requiring reproductive care—a policy enacted by the Biden administration in the wake of *Dobbs*. Tuberville's blockade came amid the wars between Russia and Ukraine *and* between Israel and Palestine. It was perhaps the greatest legislative self-own of the year. Hundreds and hundreds of senior leaders in the U.S. military were left uncertain of whether they'd be promoted, where they would live, or where they'd be enrolling their kids in school. Which was not only unethical, it was monumentally stupid.

Tuberville's goal in paralyzing the country's military was to change President Biden's abortion policy, which was never going to happen—especially following a raft of electoral wins in 2022 and 2023 that reaffirmed the Democrats' commitment to fighting to protect reproductive freedom. Lloyd Austin, U.S. secretary of defense, said, "This sweeping hole is undermining America's military readiness." Because nothing proves a pro-military posture quite like unilaterally immobilizing its leaders. Finally, on December 20, 2023, Tuberville caved and gave these families their lives back, having earned nothing but a black eye from the entire ordeal.

Shocking nobody, Trump also exploited the military while pretending to bolster it with his lies.

In 2023, he essentially teased out the suggestion that the chairman of the Joint Chiefs of Staff, Mark Milley, be executed. Executed.

These are the types of demands—against leaders, countrymen— that he has normalized. And why did he call for his death? In retribution for Milley having reassured his Chinese counterpart of the stability of the U.S. during Trump's efforts to illegally retain the presidency, and for expressing concern that Trump might provoke a military conflict with Iran as a pretense to remain in office.

This was a bridge too far for the former president, who called Milley treasonous and stated on Truth Social that talking behind the president's back was a matter "so egregious that, in times gone by, the punishment would have been DEATH!" Yes, how dare anybody fathom the idea that Trump might take steps to cling to power? How dare anybody suggest that he might not have solemn respect for the military? Certainly not the same Trump who called fallen veterans "losers" and refused to acknowledge John McCain as a war hero: "I like people that weren't captured."

It bears noting that not one member of the Trump family has served in the military.

AS FOR THE POLICE, WE NEED LOOK NO FURTHER THAN January 6, 2021, and its aftermath to see how MAGA Republican supporters feel about law enforcement. The relentless assaults on police officers protecting the Capitol were horrific, but so are the responses of party members and presidential candidates who have since called the attackers "tourists" or "patriots," pledging to pardon them if elected. Make no mistake: the Republican Party is more than willing to sacrifice our cops—the men and women who stood in to protect them—if it means upholding Trump's Big Lie.

Seared in many minds are the photos and videos of pro-Trump insurrectionists bludgeoning Capitol Hill police officers with the Stars and Stripes–topped flagpoles they had just been holding at the president's pregame rally. Heroic officer and now congressional candidate Harry Dunn has written about the rage he felt as he listened to Republicans who initially condemned the January 6 insurrection backtrack and revise their positions: "Congress members . . . whom I had guarded and protected through State of the Unions [and] inaugurations . . . suddenly turned on me." Knowing such about-faces were to please Trump, he continued, "It angered me that loyalty to a single individual could overwhelm otherwise decent people . . . who had fallen into the darkness and forgotten their oaths of office." This is after the lead instigator of such savagery released a video statement that day, a day he could have prevented, a day on which officers like Dunn were still being overwhelmed and battered. One officer died the following day. Four committed suicide in the days and months after.

What did Trump say to the mob? "We love you."

MEANWHILE, THE BIDEN ADMINISTRATION PASSED THE PACT Act, expanding health care and benefits for veterans exposed to burn pits, Agent Orange, and other toxins. Prior Republicans had initially signaled support for the legislation, but not this crew. They blocked the bill as retribution for Democrats attempting to pass the Inflation Reduction Act, and only relented when they were buried under an avalanche of bad press led by Jon Stewart—who stood alongside veterans in front of the Capitol, where he raged: "I'm used to the hypocrisy. I'm used to the lies. I'm used to the cowardice. But this type of cruelty toward those that we *say* we hold up as our most valued Americans? Then what are we? This is an embarrassment to the Senate, to the country, to the founders, and to all that they profess to hold dear. If this is America first, then America is fucked." He shouldn't have had to use his platform to convince the government to pay for the health care of first responders, but because of Republicans, he did. He attracted extraordinary amounts of coverage, without which those Republicans would have been perfectly content withholding care as a means of punishing Democrats for the "crime" of passing the IRA—legislation aimed at lowering health care costs and combating climate change. I know, *the horror.*

And, as COVID surged, Biden and the Democrats passed the American Rescue Plan, $10 billion of which was committed to police departments across the U.S. Not one single Republican voted for the bill, despite their insistence that they were devoted to law enforcement.

While professing their fervent support, GOP lawmakers have pushed for extreme cuts* to essential law enforcement. House Republicans threatened to defund Homeland Security, using

---

* The proposed cut to the FBI would eliminate up to 1,850 personnel, and the Bureau of Alcohol, Tobacco, Firearms and Explosives would be forced to eliminate approximately 400 positions, including more than 200 agents. The House bill also cuts funding for U.S. Attorneys by roughly 12 percent, which would eliminate approximately 1,400 positions.

that as a bargaining chip in an attempt to get Biden to sign border security legislation. Meanwhile, they elevated voices like Marjorie Taylor Greene's. As *Vice* noted in 2023, Greene said of January 6: "If Steve Bannon and I had organized that, we would have won. Not to mention, we would've been armed." A mere month later, she solemnly stated: "It will be my honor to serve my constituents and the American People on the House Committee on Homeland Security to focus on the security of the United States."

Relying on tired theatrics, she refused to vote for a budget that didn't include cuts to the DOJ and the FBI. She rarely knows what she's talking about, but she has become a leading spokesperson—for a party thoroughly unmotivated to uphold the law.

Forget about commonsense gun laws, which would protect both everyday citizens *and* the police. Most police, regardless of party affiliation, support this. But evidently there are Republicans who feel that Americans and those who protect them would not be best served by restricting the ease with which absolutely anyone can procure weapons of war.

Representatives Barry Moore, Lauren Boebert, and Andrew Clyde, along with disgraced former congressman George Santos, devoted legislative time and effort—and taxpayer dollars—to submitting a bill "to declare an AR-15 style rifle chambered in a .223 Remington round or a 5.56x45mm NATO round to be the National Gun of the United States." They wanted to make the AR-15 our national gun.

Might be a hard sell for the families of the forty thousand–plus people who died in 2023 due to gun violence.

While their slavish devotion to the quashing of gun legislation reform may feel like a longstanding tradition, it's a relatively new phenomenon—and an indication of how far the party has lunged to the right. While Republicans lean on the Second Amendment as a catchall to defeat reform, remember that even Antonin Scalia—arguably the most conservative justice on the Court in our lifetime—wrote, in his *District of Columbia v. Heller* opinion, "Like most rights, the right secured by the Second Amendment is not unlimited. . . . nothing in our opinion should be taken to cast doubt on longstanding prohibitions on the possession of firearms by felons and the mentally ill, or laws forbidding the carrying of firearms in sensitive places such as schools and government buildings, or laws imposing conditions and qualifications on the commercial sale of arms." So when Republicans *today* claim that any and all regulations are an infringement on our Second Amendment right, recognize just how extreme they've allowed themselves to become—while mass shootings surge.

These incidents, outbursts, and positions are a small sample of Republicans' failure to live up to their party's supposed dedication to supporting law enforcement—or to actually *prove* their platform, as opposed to just standing on it and shouting. Though their positions are not wholly without precedent, the difference today is in party members' willingness to flaunt an absolutely flippant disregard for the military, the police, and the constitutional rule of law that they help protect.

THE CONSTITUTION

The final brand, heard ad nauseum from the rhetoric blaring from Republicans' megaphones, is perhaps the most devastating to witness the party disregard, misuse, and trample: the Constitution.

The United States Constitution, which opens with "We the

People," predates the party system. Since its creation, it has dictated how government is meant to run if we want to remain a free and fair nation. The Framers built a government that would function, one that would enable the newly formed country to meet the challenges of the day.

The term "originalist," used by the likes of Antonin Scalia, federal judge Robert Bork, and others, then followed too passionately by dangerous architects like Leonard Leo, has become synonymous with "conservative": someone who relies on a strict interpretation of the Constitution rather than an expansive, living, evolving one. The more of an originalist a person is, the more conservative they identify as.

Except, apparently, regarding the parts of the Constitution that are inconvenient. Such as, for instance, not engaging in insurrection.

It's not enough that Republicans, like all elected officials, irrespective of party, take the oath to support and defend the Constitution. Republicans believe themselves to be *originalists*; the party that has so much reverence for the founding document that they adhere to every word of its text. Unlike those lawless, freewheeling Democrats, Republicans have dedicated themselves to the Constitution and the processes it dictates. It's their province.

And yet.

To even suggest that such fealty remains the case today is, unfortunately, hysterically far from true. Among the Constitution's most crucial passages is its call for the peaceful transfer of power. This process, once considered a given, was long exalted as a hallmark of American democracy. Abiding by this has revealed, most profoundly, that those in the highest positions of power promise to honor their oath. As such, there's a sense of bedrock patriotism attached to this extraordinary procedure and those who respect it.

Republican president Ronald Reagan acknowledged the marvel of the tradition in his first Inaugural Address:

> *To a few of us here today this is a solemn and most momentous occasion, and yet in the history of our nation it is a commonplace occurrence. The orderly transfer of authority as called for in the Constitution routinely takes place, as it has for almost two centuries, and few of us stop to think how unique we really are. In the eyes of many in the world, this every-four-year ceremony we accept as normal is nothing less than a miracle.*

Nothing less than a miracle. But Republicans took this "commonplace occurrence," this routine act of normality and global distinction . . . and trashed it. George Washington honorably and voluntarily stepped down at the end of his term. Before Donald Trump, never in the history of the country had a president refused to honor the peaceful transfer of power. That tradition, which speaks to an enduring unwillingness to submit to the forces of autocracy, remained unbroken for over two hundred years—until 2020–2021, when Trump opted instead to promote known lies about nonexistent fraud, prop up baseless theories to justify his refusal to leave office, launch a pressure campaign against his own vice president, and incite an insurrection against the seat of government.

All that tradition, all that precious history destroyed because, if we boil it down, the man is a terrible loser. The immediate response from Congress was nothing less than inspiring; despite the events of January 6, members returned to the Capitol *that night* and ensured that the certification of the Electoral College results proceeded, enabling Biden to become president—as the majority of America wanted and as the Electoral College vote dictated.

Nothing encapsulates Trump's disdain for the Constitution more neatly than his rejection of a peaceful transfer of power after losing an election (and knowing it). He has continued his assault on the Framers' vision for the country; let us keep in mind that he suggested terminating the Constitution. So there's really no need to hypothesize about whether he gives a shit about our founding document.

Members of both parties initially acknowledged his betrayal, which is unsurprising, given that the fear for their lives was felt in a bipartisan manner. Appallingly, the shared recognition of Trump's deception just . . . evaporated. An outrageous number of Republicans have retrospectively accepted or distorted the reality of the insurrection.

That's a tricky one to square. How could the GOP predicate its identity on a fierce and rigid commitment to the Constitution, then *stand back and stand by* as their leader continued to staunchly refuse to concede?

Trump tipped over one of the party's purported pillars of righteousness. And still the majority of Republicans decided that they could ignore the gallows that had been erected in front of the Capitol to hang the vice president. They scuttled away from the reality of Trump masterminding the coup faster than Senator Josh Hawley scurried from the insurrectionists to whom he had just raised a fist in shameless solidarity.

Disrespecting the Constitution and the rule of law becomes especially potent and frightening when we consider that there are Americans who have a system of belief centered on a baffling fidelity to Trump; who cheer like maniacs at a rodeo when he asserts that he will only be "a dictator" on "day one," and who seemingly will follow him anywhere. That includes a hypothetical fascist movement with him as that dictator and the Constitution as—at best—a dispensable relic.

MEANWHILE, ON THE THIRD ANNIVERSARY OF JANUARY 6, BIDEN expressed pride in his win. Not because he received more votes (though of course he did, by a margin of millions). It was because "ordinary citizens, state election officials, the American judicial system had put the Constitution first and sometimes at their peril—*at their peril*. Because of them, because of you, the will of the people prevailed, not the anger of the mob or the appetites of one man."

IN 2012, CONSTITUTIONAL SCHOLARS NORM ORNSTEIN AND Thomas Mann wrote, in their unfortunately prophetic *It's Even Worse Than It Looks*,* that in American politics, the Republican Party had become "an insurgent outlier—ideologically extreme; contemptuous of the inherited social and economic policy regime; scornful of compromise; unmoved by conventional understanding of facts, evidence, and science; and dismissive of the legitimacy of its political opposition."

And indeed, modern Republican strategy is at war with Democratic efforts, at war with facts, and at war with the Constitution. Their historical efforts to unsettle American trust in government; their relentless attempts to attack and undo the welcoming of immigrants, who have actually made America great; their myopic disregard for the hallowed setting of the Capitol;

---

* Their 2016 paperback was updated to read *It's Even Worse Than It Was*.

the irresponsibility on display during House Speakership debacles; the unending fuss about how the government *they* wreck doesn't work; the deafening contempt for their own colleagues; and finally, the campaign to forgo the whole "liberty for all" business . . . all of that, either literally or in spirit, repudiates the Constitution and is sharply at odds with its design.

"Party of the Constitution," as with other Republican branding, is a pretense of moral leadership. It's astonishing how long such an antidemocratic party has legitimized itself through shared lies and hypocrisies . . . and equally shocking that it continues to do so. But it's not just the collective brands, echoed through decades, that have proven to be shallow falsehoods. The individual politicians, elected to govern and represent (but then perhaps put through some terrifying filter of their party's machinery), cannot be trusted to deliver the truth.

Don't take my word for it. Take theirs.

3

THE POST-HYPOCRISY PARTY

In 2022, the Lincoln Project put out an ad that compiled commentary from Senator Lindsey Graham, underscoring how faithful members of the GOP are to their word. It opens with his well-known request: *I want you to use my words against me.*

Okay, Lindsey . . .

You know how you make America great again? Tell Donald Trump to go to hell. (2015)

I think he's crazy. (2016)

Donald is like being shot in the head. If Donald Trump carries the banner of my party, I think it taints conservatism for generations to come. (2016)

The leader of the Republican Party, Donald Trump, is the most consequential Republican since Ronald Reagan. (2022)

He's a race-baiting, xenophobic religious bigot. (2015)

No, I don't think he's a xenophobic, race-baiting religious bigot. (2018)

You know what concerns me about the American press is this endless, endless attempt to label the guy some kind of kook; not fit to be president. (2017)
I think he's a kook. He's not fit to be president of the United States. (2016)

He's a jackass. (2015)
Yeah, I like the president. (2018)

And you could use my words against me, and you'd be absolutely right.

I know, I know. Lindsey Graham is low-hanging fruit. He's a known opportunist, almost exclusively driven by his desire to stay relevant. He has zero qualms about contradicting himself publicly, especially in campaigns. But that's not unusual, of course. And, as former Senator Al Franken noted, "Lindsey saw that with Trump, if he wanted to be involved, if he wanted to be a player, he had to suck up to him. So he did. And he's not alone. That's the whole Republican Party." But while Graham wears the opportunism like a fool, about-face hypocrisy has manifested far more nefariously in other Republicans.

It has perhaps been demonstrated most consequentially and powerfully over the past two decades by Mitch McConnell. He stole a Supreme Court seat from Barack Obama (and Merrick Garland) in a deeply cynical way. He pulled a one-eighty and reversed his stance about the timing of electing a justice for a lifetime position on the Supreme Court for his *own* party just a few years later. On May 28, 2019, at a Paducah Chamber of Commerce Lunch, he was asked by a member of the press, "If a Supreme Court justice was to die next year, what would you do?"

He took a leisurely sip of his drink, smiled smugly, and replied, "Oh, we'd fill it." His sinister grin remained as the room burst into laughter. And indeed, he ensured that—a mere eight days before the election, *after* early voting had begun—ultraconservative Justice Amy Coney Barrett could slide into the seat left vacant after the death of Ruth Bader Ginsburg.

In 2024, McConnell—finally serving his last term in the Senate—might seem doddering or moderate relative to his more obnoxious colleagues, but that's just a question of style. His shameless posturing as majority leader and his refusal to vote to convict Trump or hold him to account have helped persuade the fringe that they can do anything, that rules don't apply to them, and that constitutional norms can be adjusted according to personal or political convenience.

After voting to *acquit* Trump in his second impeachment trial, McConnell took to the floor and said, "Fellow Americans beat and bloodied our own police. They stormed the Senate floor. They tried to hunt down the Speaker of the House. They built a gallows and chanted about murdering the Vice President. They did this because they had been fed wild falsehoods by the most powerful man on Earth—because he was angry he'd lost an election. Former President Trump's actions preceding the riot were a disgraceful dereliction of duty." He continued, "Trump is practically and morally responsible for provoking the events of the day."

So that we're clear, that speech, grandstanding about Trump's culpability for the events of January 6, came in the immediate *aftermath* of McConnell's vote to acquit him for it.

McConnell of course couldn't convict the man he'd just acknowledged was a practical and moral criminal; so he offered a tortured justification: the trial, unfortunately, had come after

Trump was out of office. Yet the person responsible for keeping the Senate out of session for the final weeks of Trump's term was— that's right—McConnell himself. Nancy Pelosi, then Speaker of the House, had plenty to say about that in a post-verdict press conference, calling out McConnell's hypocrisy: "It is so pathetic that Senator McConnell kept the Senate shut down so that the Senate could not receive the Article of Impeachment and has used that as his excuse for not voting to convict Donald Trump."

Democratic representative John Yarmuth, who has known McConnell since they were in college, told Lawrence O'Donnell on *The Last Word* that Mitch has always followed the power play. He "doesn't care about being called hypocritical," essentially because he knows he won't be held accountable. And despite continuing to condemn Trump's abhorrent behavior, he has again endorsed him for the election.

Rank hypocrisy, and clearly not minding being labeled as such, has become commonplace within the GOP. Perhaps that's why two-faced, election-denying Mike Johnson has won power, even though most people's reaction to his being voted into the Speaker position was: "*Sorry, who?*" Nevertheless, Johnson's se-niority makes him stand out—revealing him as marginally more treacherous than others within his party, one whose words from the Trump era have managed to age worse than milk in the sun. He has put forth, on numerous occasions, that it's not just *his* contention but that of the *founding fathers* that a president should by no means be impeached by one party. "The founders of this country warned against a single party impeachment for good reason. They feared that it would bitterly and perhaps irreparably divide our nation," Johnson said during a December 2019 debate over Trump's impeachment.

And yet, lo and behold, in the waning days of 2023,

Republicans voted to open a presidential impeachment inquiry in the House by a party-line vote, with every single Republican voting in favor of the measure, including . . . Mike Johnson.

Which leads me to believe that Johnson doesn't mind being a complete hypocrite *and* doesn't mind betraying those founding fathers he crows about. Far from being deferential to the framers' intentions, he exploits them as just a convenient scapegoat to sound virtuous while barreling ahead with his abject partisan hackery.

As if Johnson's purported hard line on one-party impeachments wasn't enough, he has also firmly stated that not only is he against them, he's especially against them eleven months out from an election. "If you don't like the president, he goes on a ballot again after four years," he said in 2019. "We have an election in 11 months. Let the people decide this."

A purportedly principled stance . . . that would miraculously vanish as Johnson sought to advance the impeachment of Joe Biden—let's see—exactly eleven months before the election.

It's like Mike Johnson is begging the world to see that, in keeping with the party he represents, he stands for absolutely nothing.

The Republicans' decision to open an impeachment proceeding was, without question, a desperate attempt to create some mirage of equivalency between Joe Biden and Donald Trump, who was impeached twice by the House, first for abuse of power and obstruction of Congress (for extorting Ukraine by withholding military assistance), then for inciting an insurrection. For the former, we have firsthand testimony from officials who were *on the call*, which was not enough for Mike Johnson. For the latter, well, the world watched Trump entreat his supporters via Twitter to go to the Capitol ("Big protest in D.C. on January 6. Be there, will be wild!") and told them to "fight like hell" once they got there. Then he sat idly by for hours while they ransacked the seat of government and sought out Mike Pence and Nancy Pelosi to assassinate; that, too, was not enough for Mike Johnson. Yet despite his apparent astronomical bar for impeachment, he didn't hesitate to advance a Biden impeachment for a crime . . . that doesn't exist, bolstered by evidence . . . that doesn't exist. In fact, the Republicans who have supported the Biden impeachment effort haven't been able to offer a sound reason for their inquiry, as evidenced in this exchange between Representatives Joe Neguse, a Democrat, and Guy Reschenthaler, a Republican:

NEGUSE: *What is the specific constitutional crime that you are investigating?*

RESCHENTHALER: *High crimes, misdemeanors, and bribery.*

NEGUSE: *What high crime and misdemeanor are you investigating?*

RESCHENTHALER: *Look, once I get time, I will explain what we're looking at.*

Imagine being arrested, and when you ask the police what you've done wrong, all they can offer is, "*Wellll*, we'll let you know once we find something." Not to stray too far from my lane, but investigations generally begin *after* there's at least some modicum of evidence of a crime. Even Fox host Steve Doocy admitted on-air that House Republicans "have not connected the dots. They have not shown where Joe Biden did anything illegally."

The glaring lack of any predicate to move forward with a

Biden impeachment proceeding was made painfully clear on both sides of the political spectrum.

This is yet another example of the Republicans' shameless attempt to normalize behavior that is neither normal nor constitutionally supported. And though the GOP might think they're hurting the Democratic president, in reality, they're inflicting the most damage on themselves—by proving to America that they are unserious hacks operating an unserious operation, all in service of a cheap political win at any cost—even if that means waging a war on our constitutional order.

There's nobody more familiar with the reality of what they're doing than Representative Raskin, who served as lead impeachment manager in Trump's second impeachment. "What's amazing to me," he said, on *Inside with Jen Psaki*, moderated by the former White House press secretary and current MSNBC host, "is that you've got an overwhelming number of people in their caucus who voted against impeaching Donald Trump for inciting a violent insurrection against our own House, against the Congress, against the vice president—*we saw it* . . . but they voted no. Now they want to go ahead and launch an impeachment inquiry against Joe Biden for a crime unknown . . . so Donald Trump can say, 'Well, I might have four indictments against me across the country, eighty-eight criminal charges, and two impeachments—but this guy is being brought up on impeachment too, so we're even.'"

The sham impeachment effort against Biden proved to be an embarrassing reveal of incompetence by Republicans. They had moved to impeach based on allegations from a confidential source laid out in FBI Form 1023 (and of course you've never heard of it, which is the point; it's vague enough for Republicans to wrongly invoke it as definitive proof, recognizing that virtually no one knows enough about it to refute their claims). The 1023 document contained the false charge that the Bidens received millions of dollars in bribes to benefit Ukrainian energy company Burisma, on whose board Hunter Biden sat.

In February 2024 it was revealed that the informant who had provided this "smoking gun," Alexander Smirnov (cue a Russian villain out of an '80s movie), was lying, resulting in an indictment by the DOJ. That alone would be enough to discredit this entire process. Worse, we learned that Smirnov had been fed his bogus intel by Russian intelligence officials (so he basically *was* a Russian villain out of an '80s movie).

In other words, a hostile foreign power was able to influence the United States Congress through some useful idiot who laundered their disinformation, with the express goal of ending Joe Biden's presidency. If that wasn't bad enough, Republicans marched ahead even *after* Smirnov's allegations were debunked. Jim Jordan held a press conference, saying, "It doesn't change the fundamental facts," to which a reporter replied, "It does change the facts, because they're no longer facts."

Jordan and his colleagues will carry on this charade despite its fatal flaws because both the Republican Party and Russia benefit from their arrangement: Putin knows that Trump, as president, will undermine NATO; Trump and Republicans know Putin will help them get elected. This deal is so transparent that when I asked President Biden for his response to Trump praising the same guy who would invade Ukraine, he said, "I put as much stock in Trump saying that Putin's a genius as I do when he calls himself a stable genius."*

---

* If you thought I wasn't going to figure out a way to casually mention my interview with the president of the United States . . .

When that first impeachment against Biden didn't work out for them, or—as Raskin phrased it on the House floor in 2024—when the "madcap wild goose chase to impeach Joe Biden produced no wild geese . . . the Trump-Putin MAGA faction, headed up by the distinguished gentlelady from Georgia" Marjorie Taylor Greene, turned instead toward a "worthless trinket of a consolation prize: the opportunity to bring a slapstick impeachment drive against a Cabinet member of unimpeachable integrity who has obviously committed no treason, no bribery, no high crimes, no misdemeanors, nothing indictable."

In this case he was referring to Alejandro Mayorkas, secretary of Homeland Security. The first time they voted on his case, it was recognized as yet another farcical and baseless exercise, brought to the floor and put to a vote, where it lost: a Republican inquiry defeated in a Republican-led House. It was an embarrassing moment for the GOP, which is precisely why Greene found a way to blame it on the Democrats. She was especially heated because Johnson had preemptively suggested that he would appoint her the "manager" of the Mayorkas impeachment, which would have given her ample opportunity to hear herself speak and to take selfies with the Speaker. But once they lost, she dramatically left the chamber, then claimed to a throng of reporters that this had all been a Democratic ploy: they had *hidden* Congressman Al Green. In reality, Green had been recovering in the hospital but had taken it upon himself to make it back to the Capitol to cast his vote.

House Republicans would ultimately attempt to impeach Mayorkas for a *second* time, and were successful—only to witness the articles of impeachment fail decisively at a short-lived Senate trial. But it's also worth noting that these Republicans truly suck at getting *anything* passed. Whereas Nancy Pelosi was always famously aware of how many votes she could count on and would give herself the padding of a few votes (in case of stowaway Republicans, perhaps) and almost never brought a bill to the floor that she thought she might lose, Speaker Johnson is a bit more cavalier, remarkably less savvy, and entirely in the pocket of the former president.

The common sense that has helped sustain our union and kept our government functioning has become inapplicable to a whole half of our lawmakers. It doesn't matter how hypocritical Mike Johnson and the rest of the Republicans have been about sham impeachments, or about immigration bills that they demanded for months and then voted against. These aren't opportunities to prove or preserve integrity . . . there *is* no integrity in their process. The whole point of these charades is for them to do or say whatever they can to perpetuate their phony narrative that Biden has done something wrong—again, as a means of creating a false equivalency with Trump.

They're not interested in facts. They don't get bogged down by reality. They are merely inventing an imaginary universe and then living in that strange wormhole of bullshit until they get Trump back. This is a party that is desperate to preserve problems so that they can use them to exact revenge on Democrats and give their mad king an issue to roar about incoherently and run on.

We will endure this until November 2024—and likely beyond. Their goal, again, is merely to create the illusion of crime and crises. Do they look like absolute hacks? Yes. Will they continue anyway? Also yes. They have to maintain whatever terrifying fantasies necessary to keep their base good and angry. These are manipulation tactics happening at the hands of the very people whom voters have been groomed to trust. Republicans may claim to hate the Democrats, but frankly there is no one they have more contempt for than their own supporters.

Representative Raskin has been a front-row observer of this dramatic debasement in Republican behavior for the last eight years. He had the mixed bag of emotions that would accompany being elected on the same night as Donald Trump. They entered office together (not arm in arm, I assure you—but simultaneously) in January 2017.

"I was curious to see how Republicans who like to think of themselves as the benchmark of normality would respond to such fanaticism and instability," he said. Without speaking for the congressman, I presume he would say that they fell short of any hopeful expectations—in the way that one might "fall short" while attempting to hop across, say, the Grand Canyon.

In less than a decade, he's had to bear witness as the more sane and stable Republicans defected from their party and ultimately departed government or—far worse—conformed to what he calls "the cultishness and derangement of the Trump machinery." Raskin is well schooled in the natural conclusions of these dangerous cycles of history and has schooled many others in it. He has since become an essential eyewitness to that remarkably brief window for such extraordinary change—from the White House as Obama left it to the point where "the Republicans calling the shots are total sycophants and enablers of Donald Trump."

I asked Raskin how it's possible to compromise, fight, or govern alongside such a party—one whose members clearly have no shame and who, in the model of their indicted leader or their minority leader, are so unabashedly hypocritical. "Oh, I don't even use the language of hypocrisy to describe them," he said. "Hypocrisy is the distance between your self-proclaimed ideals and your practice. They don't have any ideals. Nobody ever called Mussolini or Pinochet or Hitler a hypocrite. That's the last thing they were. Their vice was cruelty, and a desire to dominate and control at all costs. They're a rule-or-ruin party. So hypocrisy is almost a *flattering* term to apply to them, because it suggests that they have some ideals to betray. They don't."

This devastating assessment extends beyond the House and Senate and outward toward the more extreme members of the right-wing media ecosystem. Which means that supporters are receiving deeply flawed and distorted information and consuming it as reality.

GIVEN THAT REPUBLICANS' ONLY REAL POLICY IS THIS DESIRE FOR a government steeped in dysfunction (or to make the Democrats appear dysfunctional and untrustworthy), and given, too, that the party is fundamentally opposed to democracy, the GOP is at an existential crossroads. They have allowed themselves to be controlled by a small, useless faction of hostile actors, all of whom are either unwilling to cooperate or just excessively hostile to cooperation.

When I spoke to Representative Raskin, Kevin McCarthy had recently been ousted from his speakership—but Raskin felt little pity for him. He holds him responsible for a great deal of Donald Trump's ability to tighten his stranglehold on the Republican Party. "He knew what Trump was up to. He called Trump on January 6th from his office to complain that he was being besieged by fanatics and asked Trump to call off the dogs, to which Trump famously replied, 'It's not my people, it's Antifa.' McCarthy said, 'No, they're in my office. This is not Antifa, these are your people, Mr. President.' And Trump said, 'Well, maybe they just care more about a fair election than you do, Kevin,' essentially telling him to get in line."

According to Raskin, McCarthy asked, "Who do you think you're talking to, Donald?" He wasn't trying to sound like a mob boss. He was pleading with Trump, saying, "I'm the person who's been carrying your water around here. I'm the one who's really slavishly pro-Trump." Trump couldn't have cared less. As Raskin emphasized, "He was willing for people to be killed. He didn't care if people died. He just wanted to be reinstated to the presidency."

Did McCarthy have a choice? Of course he did. Perhaps it was not an easy choice, given how long he'd had his eyes trained on becoming Speaker. But he did have a choice. And he sure made it quickly, by consciously deciding that his role would be *not* to hold accountable the former president but rather to rehabilitate his image within the Republican Party. Having been frightened for his life on January 6, McCarthy had initially denounced Trump . . . but quickly reassessed, left any pesky morals behind, and journeyed down to Mar-a-Lago to kiss the ring.

"He could have done the right thing, like Liz Cheney and Adam Kinzinger," Raskin said. "There were ten Republicans in the House and seven in the Senate who voted to impeach or convict. McCarthy could have done the right thing, but he didn't. He proved himself to be completely obsequious and invertebrate and even ended up withdrawing and opposing his *own* proposal for an independent outside 9/11-style commission to investigate what happened."

The moment Trump opposed the idea of an inquiry, McCarthy backflipped on his own proposal. Then and throughout his tenure in the House, he revealed himself as being so desperate for power that he was willing to cut any deal necessary that might help him ascend. Though I wouldn't credit him as possessing a savvy or strategic mind, he, too, served as a notable agent of dysfunction for the majority of his whiny career in government.

AFTER TRUMP BECAME PRESIDENT, THE REPUBLICAN PARTY—AS we all know, though it can't be emphasized enough—fully relinquished its identity. Slogans may have stuck around, but tangible values fell by the wayside.

For many years, the seeming glue of their party was a strong opposition to abortion. That was the primary subject that Republicans would discuss when Raskin entered Congress. "When I first got in, it was pretty much all I heard about: abortion was murder; abortion was a holocaust; abortion was the central moral drama of our times."

But that has backfired. Ever since they ostensibly got what they wanted with the *Dobbs* decision, it's become abundantly clear, in midterm and referendum votes, that the people of the United States (or roughly 70 percent of them) believe women should have the freedom to make their own choices about their body, their family, and their destiny.

After reproductive rights referendums passed in Kansas, Wisconsin, Ohio, and elsewhere, Republicans smartened up and stopped running their mouths about the issue. Gone was the righteous indignation about abortion, replaced by the quiet din of crickets chirping. Soon the party moved on to immigration, though they've made it evident that they're not actually interested or invested in solving the problems at the border so much as just complaining about how little is being done, while leaving Trump room to campaign on the issue.

I interviewed Senator Chris Murphy, who helped write the border bill that Republicans demanded (before balking once they realized that it would mean losing a potent issue ahead of the election). He said, "I actually think this flips the politics of the border. I think this probably *was* going to be a tough issue for Democrats; I think it's a much less tough issue now, because we have a bipartisan bill that would've controlled the border. Republicans are against it only because they don't actually want to fix the problem and they kind of admitted it in front of everybody."

The Republicans are putting on a clinic about what happens when the dog catches the car. They pushed to outlaw abortion . . . until they got it, and suddenly went mum on the issue. They pushed for conservative border legislation . . . until they got it, and suddenly balked at a solution. While it's unclear what the next big issue will be, it's already plenty clear that it'll be less about the merits and more about the overall strategy: they need *something* to run their mouths about, as it's essential that they—and Trump—have a topic they can dine out on to provoke their base's contempt, frustration, and most importantly, votes.

Such topics aren't as easy to come by as one might assume. For all the talk of how divided we are as a nation, several of the people I spoke with for this book mentioned that most Americans have more shared values than we think, or more than is portrayed. Republicans are numerically in the minority. Which is why they've adapted to the manipulation of minority rule. They're at their best not when change needs to be conceived of and consciously made but when they can position themselves in opposition to Democrats. They are relentless contrarians.

Out of the last nine elections for president, Republicans have won the popular vote all of . . . once. But just as they have a bag of brands, they also have a bag of tricks for elections.

"Those tricks all involve antidemocratic mechanisms either built into the Constitution or that they have created outside of it," Raskin explains. "Some of the constitutional ones are the

Electoral College, which is obviously this obsolete artifact from the eighteenth century, but it's given us five popular-vote losers for president, twice in this century alone, in 2000 and in 2016. The Republicans understand that that dramatically favors them, both because they're a minority party but also because it specifically inflates the power of the less-populous states. . . . So the Electoral College favors the Republicans just the way the U.S. Senate favors the Republicans. Then there are extra-constitutional mechanisms that they have evolved, like voter suppression tactics, or like throwing people off of the rolls if they haven't voted in an election, or like the massive closure of precinct polling places across the country and the increasing difficulty of registering a vote."

This is where Republicans thrive: in manipulating institutions like the Electoral College, in gerrymandering congressional and state legislative districts, in imposing voter suppression tactics, in preserving the filibuster. Like their leader, they are a party that specializes in the techniques of antidemocracy.

And Americans have become bizarrely complicit in allowing different standards for Democrats and Republicans. Marc Elias spoke to this nonsensical, unconstitutional division: "I recoil at the arguments we so often hear. People will say, 'Well, Joe Biden needs to win by enough that Donald Trump can't even contest the election.' What kind of election system is it when one candidate gets to win by a little whereas the other has to win by a lot? Or people say, 'We can't have the disqualification of Donald Trump because people will threaten another January 6th.' What kind of system is that? You can't have a political system where one side has to be adults and the other does not."

Yet this is the party system we find ourselves with. Somehow it's been baked in. Radical Republicans, in particular, are going to throw their toys around and have temper tantrums and that's just the way it is. It's equally understood that Democrats have to be adults about whatever decisions come their way, good or bad.

We need to stop accepting as inevitable or normal that Republicans would launch another insurrection or violently react if, for example, Trump gets a ruling that he and they don't agree with.

Elias proposed a game of hypotheticals. Imagine this scenario: "The Supreme Court of the United States ruled to overturn two centuries of precedent in saying that the right to bear arms under the Second Amendment was absolutist and could not be restricted, that it had nothing to do with a well-regulated militia, and that we are now dealing with the epidemic of gun violence that we have as a result. Imagine if people who opposed that ruling simply said, 'We're not going to accept that. We're going to confiscate guns. We're going to send our police in to grab guns from people.' Imagine what the reaction would be." If guns don't bother you, he offered an additional scenario. "Imagine for a moment that when the U.S. Supreme Court overturned *Roe v. Wade*, which had been settled law and settled constitutional precedent for more than a generation, if people on the left had said, 'You know what? We're going to threaten states with violent reactions to this,' rather than do what people have actually done, which is to organize, to hold ballot initiatives to abide by the rule of law, to try to move state legislatures to vote anti-choice candidates out of office."

The point brings us back to our strange and damaging acceptance not just of politicians who have passed the threshold of hypocrisy but of an entire public that more or less has gotten used to this double standard. The radical right regularly threatens violence and unlawfulness as reasonable responses to not getting their way and—somehow—civil society needs to account for and be understanding of that? As Elias emphasized, "It's an affront to democracy. It's an affront to how we work in a diverse, pluralistic society where there are going to be disagreements. And, frankly, it's not to be tolerated anymore."

If it's not to be tolerated anymore, where do we go from here? How does a party trying to practice democracy in good faith, as the Democrats are, a party in which all stakeholders' and constituents' interests are represented, compete with one that's openly acting in bad faith, and whose raison d'être is expressly to prevent the government of which they are a part from functioning? How do we stand up to a party peddling grievance and sowing skepticism but with which we have to find common ground? Can our institutions of government actually solve problems if we continue down this path? Is it possible to practice democracy? Because I'm of the mind that we're past the point of simply abiding by former First Lady Michelle Obama's famous adage "when they go low, we go high."

That's an admirable stance, but it assumes that both parties are on the same field, playing the same game. Unfortunately, we're not.

Raskin explained the challenge by speaking of a professor who always taught him that "in a parliamentary setting, the progressives and liberals will be on the side of expanding freedom and democracy, but the right will be there to block it, and they're generally much better organized and much better focused in a hierarchical discipline—ready to fight. Liberals and progressives generally are not, at least until things get very bad and very serious. We may be there right now. But it is far more difficult to be a party of democracy, freedom, and equality, where a thousand flowers bloom and everybody is speaking for him- or herself, than to be in a party of natural authoritarians like the Republicans are today."

That's the scenario we're facing. Those in power, particularly the MAGA faction, truly have no program or platform of values. It is just complete submission to Donald Trump—they will do whatever he says,* regardless of how deranged he appears or how outrageous his behavior is.

As we all witnessed, Trump did not try to govern the country. He made aggressive promises, verbally assaulted any members of either party that challenged him, and, according to Raskin, "would just play footsie with Vladimir Putin, and nearly everybody in the Republican Party went along with it."

AS WE MOVE FORWARD AND TRY TO REDEFINE WHAT PROGRESS means today and attempt to figure out how to make our government tenable, we have to be clear about our definition of democracy. It's the institutional structure dictated by the Constitution, the Congress, the freedom of press, and the courts.

But democracy is also a spirit; it's that idea of America that Biden reiterates. Whether you adhere to every letter of it or view that spirit as an ongoing, fluid, and dynamic project, both aspects of democracy—the institution and the idea—have to be defended.

Our democracy can only exist if all of its members agree to participate. And if that seems like a tenuous framework, it is. In a two-party system, all it takes is one of the two sides deciding that they're no longer interested in abiding by the rules before the system crumbles. We were fortunate that *just enough* Republicans (Mike Pence and Brad Raffensperger, among others) were willing to put their allegiance to the country over their allegiance to Trump after January 6. The system held—but just barely. If the vast majority of the GOP had had its way in 2020, Joe Biden wouldn't have become president, despite election deniers failing to

---

* The RNC didn't even bother writing a new platform in 2020 in their blind deference to Trump and whatever errant thought might fall out of his mouth at any moment.

prove widespread fraud in any of the more than sixty court cases they brought following the election. It put on full display just how precarious our system really is.

What about Republicans, then? Is there any hope for them? Any salvageability for a party that still has a smattering of reasonable adherents who recognize how profoundly toxic Trump is? In the mid-nineteenth century, the Republican Party came in as a third party that replaced the Whigs. It started as an admirable, progressive innovation. You'd be hard-pressed to imagine it today, but the party once represented those in favor of freedom, unions, and immigration. Opposition was always in their blood, but that stance once translated into defiance of slavery and hostility toward the Confederate states. Abraham Lincoln was indeed their first president, helming their victory in the Civil War. And those original members refused to recognize the right of states and territories to practice slavery.

That's far from who they are today, when everything they once stood for has been turned upside down—when they have become, as Raskin sees it, "a cloak of an authoritarian personality wrapped around the little finger of one madman. It's a shrinking minority party that depends on antidemocratic devices to survive."

Which raises the question: Why go the route of authoritarianism? In part because, as Raskin believes, the political ideology of pre-Trump Republicanism was pretty much exhausted from as far back as Mitt Romney's campaign for president in 2012.

Authoritarianism "was essentially a kind of hailed protest against the social solidarity commitments that the Democratic Party has succeeded with," Raskin says. The Republicans "kept talking about dismantling Social Security or Medicare or Medicaid. They were thriving on culture-war issues like abortion and contraception and anti–gay rights."

As these became minority views across the country, however, Republicans began losing elections.

There's wide consensus that 2012 was a watershed in Republican politics. Marc Elias also invoked the year as a turning point for the GOP as we know it today. "There is this document called the RNC autopsy. It was put together after the 2012 election. And it is basically the Republican Party saying, We need to change our ways. We need to attract young voters and minority voters, particularly Hispanics. And we need to adopt a pathway to citizenship, we need to soften on abortion. So out of that comes Jeb Bush. The Bush family had a connection with Hispanics—Jeb was married to a Hispanic woman.

"And there's this idea that there can be this reemergence of this much softer version of conservatism. And he loses to Donald Trump. What happens then is the Republicans go *all in* on the opposite. So you go from this bipartisan consensus, to basically making voting technocratically easier, to an absolute all-out war on voting that starts with Donald Trump literally in 2016, the day after the election, saying that the reason why he didn't win the popular vote is because three million illegal aliens voted in California. And it just goes from there. That's, to me, the tragedy of where we are from a democracy standpoint."

Donald Trump revived and redirected the Republican Party backward, using "good old-fashioned racism and immigration bashing," Raskin explained. "And then this new breed of extremist authoritarian politics followed. He brought in a lot of alienated people on these authoritarian impulses." These disenfranchised people somehow feel that he is speaking on their behalf. A reporter asked Raskin, "Do you think anybody can beat Donald Trump in the Republican Party?" Which, for him, was akin to being asked, "Do you think anybody can beat David Miscavige in the Church of Scientology?"

Cult leaders are exceptionally hard to topple, no matter how they behave or how many felony charges they have against them. Even if one of Trump's doomed-from-the-start primary opponents had managed to get a competing number of delegates, the fear and assumption is that he would just divorce himself (he has a decent amount of experience with such matters) from the party. He's never shared any core ideology with party members, other than obsessing about power and money, and would oppose them anyway.

"So they're trapped at this point by their own acquiescence and obeisance to Donald Trump," said Raskin.

I understand the catch-22 for Republicans: getting elected starts with Trump, to whom they need to prove themselves adequately loyal, but the more they tie themselves to him, the less electable they become. We look at the 2022 midterm cycle as a stinging defeat for Republicans, but the lesser-known reality is that Republicans *did* perform quite strongly—in races where the candidates weren't in the mold of Donald Trump; the problem* is that most of their candidates *were* in the mold of Donald Trump. Republicans flipped four House seats in the big blue liberal bastion that is New York. Republicans held on to a raft of swing seats in the other big blue liberal bastion that is California. Georgia secretary of state Brad Raffensperger (whose "perfect" phone call with Trump on January 2, 2021, in which Raffensperger was pressured to "find" 11,780 votes) won reelection. It was the candidates running expressly on Trump's MAGA agenda who lost: Herschel Walker, Dr. Oz, Blake Masters, Kari Lake, Don Bolduc, Doug Mastriano, Kristina Karamo, J.R. Majewski, Tudor Dixon, and (because time is a flat circle and we live in hell) Sarah Palin.

But Trump still enjoys the power of the extreme Republicans

---

* And the gift . . .

who continue bending over backward to give it to him. For years, they've been falling all over themselves and each other to ensure that he remains the leading figure on the right, thereby entrenching the catch-22 that's (mercifully) responsible for cycle after cycle of Republican losses.

With each abuse, Trump, like an addict seeking a new high, is emboldened to continue pushing the limits of what he can get away with. And the Republicans, far from staging the necessary intervention, enable his behavior and facilitate the weakening of their own party. The only explanation fathomable, given their rush to defend him over what seems to the rest of us like voluntarily walking into the mouth of an active volcano, is that there is freedom in not being subjected to Trump's unforgiving shame.

In late 2023, I interviewed Raskin's House Oversight Committee colleague, Representative Alexandria Ocasio-Cortez, who can speak with authority on Republican lunacy thanks to her close proximity to fellow committee members like Jim Jordan, James Comer, and Marjorie Taylor Greene. She wondered whether "the hypocrisy itself strengthens them, because they are showing that this is actually not about values; it's a dog whistle to their supporters that this is actually just a show, and that what this is really about is power. And us getting power and us doing what we want."

Consider the world of possibility that opens up to these Republican officials once they recognize that hypocrisy no longer matters. No longer restrained by the threat of being exposed or chastened, they can contradict themselves, they can flip-flop, they can flaunt double standards, they can prevent the passage of legislation that they themselves demanded.

Post-hypocrisy, and with shame out of the equation, they're free to do what they actually want to do, which is to consolidate power for themselves. What we perceive as a weakness is actually one of their greatest, albeit amoral, assets. They no longer need to waste time with the pretense of honesty and integrity; now they can dedicate themselves to a rabid, relentless, shameless pursuit of power.

RECOGNIZING THEIR DESPERATION FOR POWER AND THE lengths to which they will go to get it, we're not doing ourselves any favors to deny that if we don't build a large coalition of people to reject it, the Republicans' pathetic servility could very easily result in fascist politics returning to the Capitol. The fight for democracy cannot be won by a few heroes, or even a few groups of them. "If we fight, if we organize, if we mobilize the huge numbers of people who prefer democracy to tyranny, then the defense of our institutions is viable," Raskin said. "So we've got our work cut out for us, there's no doubt. But democracy lives in the struggle for democracy.

"This is an all-hands-on-deck moment. We need anybody who wants to stand up for constitutional democracy to join us," Raskin entreats. "We need to send the message throughout our society that this is way beyond the normal push-and-pull politics of Democrats and Republicans. We're really talking about the defense of our constitutional order against a political party that is attacking it from the outside and that does not recognize the rightful claims of our Constitution and our institutions."

The eagerness of extreme Republicans to abandon those democratic standards and establish their own rules is perhaps strategic, perhaps desperate, or perhaps an inevitable consequence of Trump's narcissistic influence on our political landscape. Regardless, it's the reason "authoritarianism" has become an unfortunate buzzword to explain what has happened to the Republican Party.

Raskin explained that our present batch of Republican lawmakers "do have an authoritarian mindset of taking power by any means necessary. The hallmark of the authoritarian parties is a refusal to accept the results of democratic elections when they don't go their way. Another hallmark is a refusal to disavow—or an enthusiastic embrace of—political violence as an instrument for achieving power."

In May of 2024, Republican officials began flaunting their unwillingness to commit to accepting the election results. Senator Tim Scott from South Carolina, vying for Trump's vice presidential slot, appeared on *Meet the Press* and was asked if he would accept the election results, regardless of who wins. Six times, he refused to do so, opting instead to offer, "At the end of the day, the 47th president of the United States will be President Donald Trump." Days later, Senators Lindsey Graham and JD Vance were asked the same question. Both took a slightly different tack, offering to accept the election results, albeit with conditions: Graham said he would accept them provided there's no "massive cheating," and Vance said he would accept them assuming they're "free and fair." Of course, Republicans' perception of a "free and fair" election, devoid of "massive cheating" has proven subjective at best. We accept these tenuous reassurances at our own peril.

Americans have developed a tendency, especially in the Trump era, to quickly grow accustomed to whatever fresh political hell has befallen us as the new normal. But one of our two major political parties is openly embracing authoritarianism—in a country whose entire identity is predicated on freedom, democracy, and the Constitution. And they're led like groveling bootlickers by a racist, xenophobic con man found liable for both civil fraud and sexual assault in New York courtrooms—as he awaits four different trials for eighty-eight felony charges* for which he's been indicted. As

---

* See Appendix A.

president, he lost the greatest number of jobs in modern U.S. history, oversaw a contraction of the economy, presided over the worst pandemic response in the industrialized world, and (despite his promises that his fans would tire of all the winning) lost the House, Senate, and White House. He is obsessed with showerheads and flushing toilets, has suggested that World War II hasn't happened yet, and claimed on at least a dozen occasions either that he defeated Barack Obama or that Obama is still in office. He spends his time infatuated with conspiracy theories about his own election results, trial results, and even golf results, unable to accept the fact that he is a loser. He has bilked his supporters for hundreds of millions of dollars despite swooping into office on promises that he would be "greedy for our country." He promised to release from prison the insurrectionists who stormed the Capitol on January 6, vowed to terminate the Constitution, and argued that a president should be given total immunity under any circumstances—implying that this should apply even in an instance of potentially having a political opponent assassinated. He equated counterprotesters with neo-Nazis at Charlottesville and offered a rallying cry to the Proud Boys during a nationally televised presidential debate. He told over thirty thousand lies in office, keeping fact-checkers exceptionally busy as they tracked an average of roughly twenty-one erroneous claims per day over the course of his presidency, culminating in an absolute delusion fest just before the 2020 election, when the *Washington Post* cited 503 false or misleading claims made in one day. He still boasts that he passed a very basic test intended to detect the onset of dementia. It would be impossible—*impossible*—to find a more vulnerable, pathetic, target-rich political opponent.

Amid this bounty of horrors, *how are the Democrats responding?*

4

CONTINUED ON NEXT BUMPER STICKER

Imagine this: one party takes on the creation of nationwide health care reform; puts together a massive, multipronged infrastructure bill; addresses climate change; and establishes a successful rescue plan that facilitates the swiftest economic recovery on the planet in the wake of a global pandemic.

The other party fails about a hundred times to repeal that health care reform, fails at building infrastructure, fails to acknowledge climate change, and primarily throws itself headlong into a movement led by a man who rails about a stolen election—while struggling mightily to spell the word "stollen."*

Which one *should* have a harder job conveying the priorities of their brand?

Don't worry: I'm not going to argue that Democrats are flawless messengers, or that there is no truth whatsoever to the widely held conviction that the left struggles with promoting themselves and conveying their accomplishments. When trying to understand

---

* *What is stollen? The German cake that Donald Trump keeps accidentally promoting through misspelled posts*: Stollen is a Christmas delicacy consisting of dried fruits, nuts, and powdered sugar that originated in Germany. (*The Independent* UK, August 23, 2023.)

why this is the case, those reasons are unpacked with optimum flair by someone who not only worked within government but satirized it professionally from without. Al Franken had a singular path to the Capitol. He's the only Senate Judiciary Committee member in history to have also portrayed a member of that committee in a nationally televised comedy sketch. His thirty-five years parodying politics on *Saturday Night Live* and elsewhere give him a unique perspective on the strengths and pitfalls of political messaging. He moved on from writing for the legendary show to winning a seat in the Senate, landing him right in the thick of the decisions and the debates, the bureaucracy and the bullshit.

Working from outside and inside the Capitol, Franken is well versed in the longstanding criticism that Democrats aren't particularly skilled at branding themselves. In exploring why this has been our tradition and why the judgment has persisted, he explained wryly, "All our bumper stickers end with 'continued on next bumper sticker.'" By contrast, he noted that "Republican issues are very short: 'Low taxes.' 'Less bureaucracy.' 'Fewer regulations.' Those are pretty simple, and they resonate with people, and that's an advantage. Our issues are harder to explain and take a little bit longer."

Which makes sense: Democrats are the party of progress. Inherent in that ambition are the policies and plans required to achieve forward movement for the nation. But far from regarding that as a weakness, Democrats wear it as a point of pride. Elizabeth Warren's 2020 unofficial presidential campaign motto was "I've got a plan for that." And she wasn't alone that year in what *Guardian* editor Betsy Reed dubbed the "ideas primary":

> *Bernie Sanders has rolled out a package of proposals to "rebuild rural America" and released legislation to cap credit card interest rates at 15%. Kamala Harris has come out with a bill to financially*

assist public defenders. Cory Booker has proposed sweeping reforms to the nation's gun laws. Kirsten Gillibrand has vowed to only nominate Supreme Court justices who would uphold Roe v Wade. *Amy Klobuchar has laid out a $100bn plan to combat drug and alcohol addiction and improve mental healthcare.*

Reading that, the policy wonk in me still gets inspired by the potential for possibility. How could anyone *not* want this? And not just want to witness the achievement of such goals—but also to be a part of the process of restoring a broken nation; of rolling up our sleeves and creating the change we so desperately need?

But however impressive they sounded to young idealistic voters, it wouldn't take long before Elizabeth Warren's brilliant lectures about how she intended to break the political influence of market-dominant companies were drowned out by the brutish slogans bellowed by the Republican nominee and incumbent president. Donald Trump and the more feverish of his MAGA followers had been repeating the same fighting words for four years: *BUILD THE WALL! LOCK HER UP! DRAIN THE SWAMP!*

Deep dives into the intricacies of empowering workers through accountable capitalism, evidently, do not catch fire among most voters, nor are they as easily regurgitated as the three-word chants Trump barks like a fascist Mother Goose. His words have stuck, owing partially to the fact that they're concise and aggressive. As to why Trump hasn't updated his repertoire or followed through on *any* of them: he has no legitimate policies to unpack or promote. He simply babbled words that he thought sounded good. He also repeated them *so. damn. much.* Repetition is a powerful tool.

The goal for Trump was to repeat his slogans so much that they became conventional wisdom. That's a strategy that the right has employed with great success for decades. Back in 2004, *The*

Daily Show's Jon Stewart* explained, "Conventional wisdom is the agreed-upon understanding of an event or person. *John Kerry is a flip-flopper. George Bush has sincere heartland values . . . and is stupid.* What matters is not that the designation be true, just that it be agreed upon by the media, so that no further thought has to be put into it. So how is conventional wisdom arrived at? For instance, let's take the example of the addition of John Edwards to the Democratic ticket. *I don't know how to feel about that. I don't know what it means*," Stewart mused.

Cut to: a CNN reporter stands in front of the White House displaying a packet of papers to the camera. "This is twenty-eight pages from the Republican National Committee," she explains. "It says, 'Who is Edwards?' Starts off by saying, 'a disingenuous, unaccomplished liberal.' We also saw from the Bush-Cheney camp that they had released talking points to their supporters."

Back to Stewart: "Talking points! That's how we learn things. But how will I absorb a talking point, like 'Edwards and Kerry are out of the mainstream,' unless I get it jackhammered into my skull? That's where television lends a hand!"

Cut to: a montage of half a dozen Bush-Cheney surrogates parroting the words "way out of the mainstream" like pull-string dolls. "He stands way out of the mainstream. Way out of the mainstream. Stands so far out of the mainstream. He is out of the mainstream. Out of the mainstream. He's well out of the main-stream." The same words, repeated over and over and over, getting jackhammered into our skulls.

---

* If you thought I would get through this book without at least once invoking our north star for New York–born/New Jersey–raised Jewish liberals, think again.

When Stewart reappears on the screen, he offers, "I think they're out of the mainstream." The segment ends with him saying: "Talking points: they're true . . . because they're said a lot."

Somehow a segment recorded two decades ago is even more applicable today. And the strategy of repetition fostering conventional wisdom has become even more relevant in the meantime.

But Trump has managed to take this strategy a step further; he doesn't just use repetition to sear his slogans into the cerebral cortexes of his supporters, he very likely uses it to convince *himself* that his own lies are true.

He's repeated so many times the baseless assertion that his call with Brad Raffensperger was perfect* that I wouldn't be surprised if he actually believes his revisionist version of the truth (that version, by the way, will be of little import to the jury in Fulton County, Georgia). Whether wittingly or not, that's how committed to the tool of repetition Trump is; he'll wield it against himself. Which suggests that the Democrats' thoughtful policy proposals and plans are no match for the zombie army of Trump supporters who are still out there chanting *BUILD THE WALL* and *DRAIN THE SWAMP* and *STOP THE STEAL* as mechanically as they can recite their own phone numbers.

Revising language as a means of covering up reality and coercing voters is not a sparkly new idea within the party Trump claims as his own. Earlier, more disciplined Republicans were fed crucial assistance in reframing language to make it simpler and more compelling to voters. Mehdi Hasan mentioned how valuable political

---

* Not to be confused with Trump's *other* "perfect" phone call, in which he attempted to extort Ukrainian president Volodymyr Zelensky for dirt on Joe Biden ahead of the 2020 election, for which he was impeached.

pollster and messaging whiz Frank Luntz was in early memos to George W. Bush; he advised the president that "the best way to deny climate change was to call Bush's White House policy the 'Clear Skies Initiative.'" Bush issued an executive order under that name. "An Orwellian label," wrote the Brookings Institution, as Luntz's verbal bait-and-switch had obscured a fossil fuel industry's wish list by casting it as an environmentally friendly movement.

Luntz helped develop the language to sell the Republicans' 1994 "Contract with America." He wrote weekly strategy memos for Senator Trent Lott's advisory group during Clinton's impeachment trials, then worked behind the scenes in debate prep sessions and in the halls of Congress, advising Republicans on issues of language. Although he would claim otherwise, he's a spin doctor, a smear professional, and a master at misrepresenting policies to sway public opinion. He is the mastermind reframer behind rebranding the estate tax or inheritance tax as the "death tax"* to dissuade people from voting for it. (The "death tax" sounds far more relatable; after all, everyone dies. But not everyone dies with the more than $13 million that's shielded from taxation upon death, which is the threshold in 2024.) He recommended that Republicans avoid talking about *drilling* in the Arctic wildlife preserve and instead call the activity *energy exploration*. He advised that casino *gambling* be cast as *gaming*. And he urged that *global warming* be recast as *climate change*, because—as he explained to Terry Gross on NPR's renowned show *Fresh Air*—the new label "creates less hysteria."

A great deal of rebranding came out of Luntzian messaging in the early 2000s, and much of it is still around today, contributing to the lingering illusion that Republicans, on the whole, are naturally

---

* A total misrepresentation, as the tax was for people who inherit an estate worth more than $2 million.

adept at branding. In large part they have, to borrow a line from Sarah Palin, just continued to "put lipstick on a pig." As Hasan states, "They've taken some of the worst policies and managed to dress them up as if they're for you." Trump never bothered with reframing or with lipstick, which many Americans misinterpreted as him being refreshingly honest.

On the other side, the Democrats' propensity for wonkiness is systemic: "This is a party of technocrats," Hasan explained. "It's a party of lawyers. It's a party of people who are much more comfortable producing hundred-page briefing books and multiple-page memos with headings and subheadings. We saw that in 2016: Hillary Clinton was the epitome of that candidate. Very smart, very organized, had a raft of detailed proposals on childcare,* but Trump said, 'Build a wall, ban Muslims, lock her up.' And that's what people remember. No one remembers the sixteen-page childcare proposal."

Campaigns have a refrain that suggests that if you're spending too much time explaining, you're losing. A lot of Democratic policies seem to require the sixteen-page treatment of data and detail, which inevitably makes them dense, less accessible, and in need of a substantive explanation about how we might reach the end goal. But *if we really drill down and break this into the major avenues of campaign messaging over the last decade and take note of how those interstates, if you will, have drastically altered the world of news traffic, by which I mean the pace of messaging, we see a trope emerging that has caused people to take the off-ramp in the nascent digital era, when peop—* and you see, by overexplaining, or being verbose, you lose. If not votes, certainly attention.

Given my work, I'm no stranger to shrinking attention spans.

---

* And was criticized for being overprepared.

Even the concept of this book is antithetical to the muscle I've built creating content. My entire career in the independent media space has been a ferocious battle for eyeballs in the overcrowded black hole that is the internet. The fact that you are this far into this book stands in aggressive conflict with everything I've ever known about consumers, which is that every second of attention has to be hard-fought and won.

That's not an exaggeration—I can see the second-by-second viewer retention analytics of every video I post on YouTube; I know how many tens of thousands of viewers swipe off or click away every moment. To that end, I'm hyper-aware that every second I can keep a viewer's attention is a privilege, and that I'm not entitled to anyone's time even if earlier videos I created garnered a lot of views. That's the reality of digital media. Consumers, viewers, and voters are more impatient and more in need of being instantly hooked or gratified than ever before.

One obstacle to immediacy, noted by both Franken and Jen Psaki, is the language many Democrats use: it tends to be inaccessible. As a result, the brand has suffered by *not* being the party for regular people who are frustrated with the system or are struggling to get by; rather, it is perceived as the party of elites. Psaki refers to "an overreliance on more complicated language, as though it's going to make you sound smarter. But actually what it does is it makes people turn you off."

She cites those who reference the Paris Agreement* in discussions of global warming (which, thanks to Luntzian branding, is now

---

* It's important to remember that, in this scenario, Republicans did not have to worry about explaining the Paris Agreement using *any* language or approach, because Trump made the wildly irresponsible, senseless decision to withdraw from it during his presidency. On Biden's first day in office as president, he officially brought the U.S. back into the agreement.

widely referred to as climate change). Many Americans are unfamiliar with the 2015 accord and don't have the luxury of being able to spend time learning about it because, say, they're trying to get their asthmatic kid to school and then to the doctor. "You know how you should talk to *that person* about climate change?" Psaki asked. "Talk about how it's causing people to have asthma. There are Democrats who *are* very good at this, but there is also a little bit of an addiction to elite language with far too many people."

One person who does not fall into the trap of using ornate rhetoric is Joe Biden. Psaki identified this quality as his superpower: he's accessible. He's from Scranton, his walls are not adorned with degrees from highbrow colleges, and he was once the poorest senator. He's the ideal person to push back on the notion that Democrats are unrelatable. Biden is not a fancy speechifier; and his lack of pretension, to many, makes him more believable and trustworthy. He will not deliver the consistently rousing, uplifting speeches that President Obama did; nor will he break down complex subjects fluidly, the way President Clinton did. Biden speaks in ways that make people feel heard, seen, and understood. It's a gift and a strength. His hard-won empathy and his sense of humor were in part developed over his many decades spent riding Amtrak between Wilmington and DC, chatting with fellow commuters. Psaki also attributes some of his superpower to the fact that he "goes to church every Saturday, then comes back to the White House and says, 'Nobody understands our economic plan, or our masking policy,' or whatever it may be. It grounds him."

THERE ARE EXCEPTIONS, AND OTHER DEMOCRATS WHO HAVE gotten it right. It certainly isn't beyond us. Franken cites "We All

Do Better When We All Do Better" as an ideal slogan. "It sums up what Democrats are all about and it's *just* short enough to fit on a bumper sticker." It comes from former senator Paul Wellstone, a huge source of inspiration for Franken. He contributed to Wellstone's strong grassroots campaigns (*so* grassroots that the two men met because Wellstone would go to nursing homes to reach voters, and Franken's father was part of a senior citizens' theater troupe).

"'We All Do Better When We All Do Better' was his philosophy, and I think that's the philosophy of the Democratic Party," Franken told me. "We believe that our society is stronger when everybody is doing better, as opposed to what Republicans believe, which is that it's dog-eat-dog out there and you need the competition and the struggle so that people work hard to gain advantage. That competition, they believe, fuels prosperity. That's in opposition to the complex society where We All Do Better When We All Do Better. That's the battle in ideologies."

In the arena of messaging, one of the Democrats' longtime strengths also carries a substantial challenge. "We are a bigger, broader coalition than they are; ranging from Bernie Sanders to Joe Manchin," Franken explains, referencing the two poles of the Democratic Party. "The broadness of our party is very different from the narrowness of theirs." Whereas achieving uniformity among Democrats is like trying to herd cats, Republicans don't have to contend with the same issue. Franken's point was reiterated by Psaki:

"The challenge and the gift of the Democratic Party is that it's a big umbrella. Nobody sings from the same song sheet, which is good! Embrace that! It's a much more diverse party. Believe me, it would be much easier to get a bunch of old white men with conservative views to sing from the same song sheet."

It is, and they do.

As far as "old white men" are concerned, it's worth noting that while Republicans love to cast the left as being obsessed with identity politics, most of their *own* politics is focused on white grievance. White voters made up 87 percent of the Republican Party on average over the last decade, as compared to an average of 63 percent for the Democrats. That may explain why the conspiracy known as the Great Replacement Theory (the view that society's share of white people is purposefully being diminished by non-whites for political gain) has emerged from the darkest corners of the right-wing ecosystem and entered the mainstream. Former Fox host Tucker Carlson normalized the concept by invoking it on more than four hundred of his shows, joined in his efforts by other Fox hosts like Laura Ingraham and Jeanine Pirro.

Or take migrant caravans, which are to American elections as red Starbucks cups are to Christmas. According to Philip Bump of the *Washington Post*, in 2018, "over the final two weeks of the midterm elections, according to closed-captioning data compiled by the Internet Archive, Fox News and Fox Business Channel each mentioned the word caravan . . . an average of almost eight times an hour. On Monday [the day before Election Day], both CNN and Fox News mentioned the caravan more than 80 times. On Tuesday, more than 40." After the election, mentions plummeted until they became virtually nonexistent.

Which is to say, Republicans deliberately use race to turn out their voters, and have done so *explicitly* for decades. The party, then, is not only physically homogeneous, but runs on a platform specifically predicated on protecting that homogeneity.

Their ideological unity, however, is not merely due to the fact that their backgrounds and circumstances tend to be more uniform than Democrats'. When it comes to the current batch of Republicans, they are notably willing to "fall in line" and endorse whatever they're told to endorse to keep the party unified . . . which, to be clear, means fulfilling Trump's desires. More often than not, that means going against their professed opinions, or against their own legislation and policy priorities they spent months working to get right.

In fact, self-opposition has been a rare point of consistency among Republicans. In 2013, as the GOP was still nursing its wounds after Mitt Romney's 44-point loss among Latinos in the 2012 presidential election and looking to make necessary inroads in that community, Marco Rubio joined a bipartisan group of seven other senators, who called themselves the Gang of Eight, and coauthored a comprehensive immigration reform bill. But opposition from House conservatives demanding more severe border security measures proved too much to bear.* Even a normal person would have trouble being heard over the clamor of these far-right lawmakers; it proved all but impossible for an invertebrate like Rubio. In the end, he was so spooked that he urged House Republicans not to pass the bill *that he himself had championed.*

We'll soon explore how, more than a decade later, Mike Johnson and his far-right cohorts demanded a conservative border bill, only to declare it "dead on arrival" in the House. The takeaway is that this is not a one-off show of cowardice; it is an embedded feature of the party. Not only are Republicans opposed to fixing any problems, but the party unites around *entrenching* those problems and eliminating real solutions. Unfortunately, these have become defining instincts of the modern GOP.

---

* A phenomenon that would prove prescient.

By contrast, Democrats' energy—on the whole—is more likely to be devoted to (as the familiar adage goes) showing rather than telling. On its face, that strategy would make sense; if you're wondering if they're pro-family, for example, what's more important: hearing them preach about that priority or expanding the child tax credit?*

The Republicans have invested a lot more resources and energy† in "telling." Former Republican lawmaker Madison Cawthorn infamously wrote a 2021 memo to his colleagues describing how his political staff was built around "comms rather than legislation." Not only are Republicans disinterested in legislating, but they're going so far as to replace legislative staff—the people who actually do the work of governing—with communications staff. Democrats can try to govern until they're (aptly) blue in the face, but just as they've been neutralized by the messaging megaphone of right-wing media, they won't be able to contend with a beefed-up messaging operation on Capitol Hill whose sole priority is to bury the left.

ANY VOID OR VACUUM IN THE POLITICAL SPHERE IS A DANGEROUS one. That's the arena where the policy of dysfunction thrives, and it is also the space that radical Republicans love to inundate with bullshit. Then, instead of moving legislation forward, instead of focusing on how We All Do Better When We All Do Better, instead of communicating and messaging at all, Democrats are forced to spend way too much time on the defensive, fending off attacks.

---

* The same child tax credit, remember, that the supposed pro-family GOP largely voted against.

† Perhaps they have a lot left over from not doing anything?

We waste time here, getting lost in the *Am not!* position on the playground. Dan Pfeiffer, former White House communications director and senior advisor to President Obama, and co-host of Crooked Media's podcasting juggernaut *Pod Save America*, spoke with me about how little gets accomplished when we get stuck in the cycle of "They say we're weak on immigration. We say we're not weak on immigration. They say we're socialists. We say we're not socialists." We may feel like we're making progress fighting back, but if we're only engaging on those terms, then we're playing on *their* turf, using *their* framing, repeating *their* talking points.

A broad goal of the few remaining clever Republicans is to make it so that you don't know what's fact and what's fiction. It's a continuation of the Steve Bannon strategy of "flood[ing] the zone with shit." The goal is to besiege the public with such a dizzying, overwhelming, disorienting barrage of disinformation that merely keeping up becomes impossible, much less discerning what's real from what's fiction. Even if Republicans can't win the messaging war, they can still make sure that everyone else loses.

The aforementioned Biden impeachment effort is a prime example. Trump was found liable for sexual assault, defamation, and fraud, and is facing eighty-eight felony charges. Republicans understood that convincing the public that Trump's hands were clean would be an impossible task. Convincing the public that Biden's were also dirty was a much lighter lift. And so even though they had failed to produce a modicum of evidence of misconduct (in particular, any that met the impeachable standard of high crimes and misdemeanors), still Republicans implied that they had—by flooding the zone with a deluge of witness depositions and 1023s and text messages and bank records and briefings.

Again, none of it contained a scintilla of proof of wrongdoing by Joe Biden, but the mere act of flooding the zone offered up the optics of corruption. It was so clear that there was no *there* there; even Steve Doocy admitted that "House Republicans had not managed to connect the dots." He acknowledged as much on *Fox & Friends*: "After dozens of interviews and over 100,000 documents released to the committees, Republicans have yet to produce any direct evidence of misconduct by Joe Biden." But the facts didn't matter; all that mattered was Republicans' ability to perpetuate a narrative that Biden was corrupt. They were not able to absolve Trump, but they sure could try to vilify Biden.

What's worse: even if their lies are exposed, it redounds to Republicans' benefit, because the conversation continues happening within the confines of their narrative. Time spent debunking Republican conspiracy theories is time not spent promoting Democrats' own narrative. So long as the news cycle is on their terrain, even if simply to expose their lies, still they derive the ultimate advantage.

"They do not care about saying anything inaccurate," Franken explained. "That's what they do, and it's especially what their spokespeople do. They'll say *anything*. So Democrats end up responding to that, and Republicans are gleeful about it." Franken contends that far from being shamed into submission when caught in a lie, they become invigorated by it.

A by-product of that dysfunction is that if Democrats take long enough to pass a bill (cheers, Kyrsten Sinema and Joe Manchin), Republicans will seize on the delay and try to destroy the legislation. Take Obamacare, for example. Obama himself conceded, "We didn't make a hard sell. We didn't have billions of dollars of commercials like some critics did. But what we said was, 'Look for yourself. See if it's good for your family.'"

The problem with not making a hard sell was that it created a vacuum that Republicans swiftly filled with a torrent of disinformation, including the infamous claim that the president's signature health care law would usher in "death panels" to decide whether patients lived or died. Franken remembers the frustration of being a part of that: "During the Obamacare rollout, every day we saw the difference between lying and telling the truth. Problem was, the truth was very complicated. We had to try to explain how Obamacare was going to work. Which takes thousands of words, because we had to explain, for example, why there was a penalty if you didn't get Medicare—which was really about making sure that everybody got in."

A tragic irony of Republicans' collective meltdown over the prospect of "death panels" in 2009 is that after *Roe* was over-turned, Kate Cox, a Texas woman whose fetus was found to have a fatal genetic condition, appeared in front of judges arguing for an exemption from the state's abortion ban—as she needed an emergency abortion. Cox had underlying health conditions, and continuing the pregnancy would have put her at high risk of medical complications and drastically reduced her chances of safely having more children. Though she was granted the exemption, Texas attorney general Ken Paxton appealed the decision to the Texas Supreme Court, which reversed the lower court's ruling. Cox was ultimately forced to leave the state to obtain care. The Republican Party's identity was predicated on its opposition to nonexistent "death panels" in 2009; by 2023, they were capitalizing on them. No one ever had to stand before a death panel because of Obamacare. But they certainly have had to because of the Republican policy decisions we're living through today.

I'll ask you to sit with that. The health care that millions of Americans now depend upon was nearly sabotaged by Republicans who inserted themselves into the debate and lied, hoping to disparage the law with their distortions. And the dire scenarios they dangled took form only once the Republicans themselves controlled the House and the Supreme Court. Conservatives so desperately wanted Obama and the Democrats to fail at providing Americans with basic health care that they dedicated years to repealing it (an effort that finally failed thanks to a mere thumb).*

"We were contending with the Bannon model of the zone being flooded with shit when they were going off about death panels or about how voting for Obamacare meant you were basically pulling the plug on Grandma," Franken said. "We lost on health care until 2018. In politics, the complicated truth loses to the very simple lie."

In 2021, this was the case with Build Back Better, the sprawling framework Biden had hoped to pass early on in his presidency to cement his legacy as a modern-day FDR. The legislation languished as it contended with immovable partisanship by Republicans (abetted by two Democrats) who vilified it relentlessly, to the point where BBB became more of a political liability than an asset. "I actually think Build Back Better was a good slogan, because it essentially said what it was talking about doing. The problem was just that it sat out there for so long because we couldn't get it passed. I blamed Manchin and Sinema for not negotiating in a way that would help it pass. But without their support, and with it just lingering and allowing people to criticize it, it became a joke and a target of attack. A very simple slogan became a bad one by virtue of the amount of time it remained on the docket. Leave anything that big out for too long and they'll turn it into a joke in and of itself," Franken lamented.

This strategy of exploiting the void isn't limited to legislation. While contending with his federal prosecutions in 2024, knowing

---

* Senator John McCain famously gave a "thumbs-down" on the Senate floor during a high-drama vote on the so-called skinny repeal of the Affordable Care Act.

that special counsel Jack Smith and his team of prosecutors couldn't comment on ongoing cases (in accordance with Justice Department policy), Trump launched a predictably relentless assault against Smith—both political and personal—in an effort to undermine the case against him. In doing so, he was able to sell a narrative (targeted at his supporters, although the impact was inevitably absorbed beyond his base) that the airtight charges against him for crimes that he had committed in full view of the public were somehow an "election interference witch hunt." By early 2024, nearly three-quarters of Republicans believed that Trump's federal prosecutions were being handled "unfairly." While this does not fall into the legislative realm (in that Smith's obligatory silence creates an inevitable void), the larger point remains the same: Republicans will take advantage of any vacuums as a means to shoehorn through their own narrative.

And so we cycle back to the toughest question: How do we fight back against a shameless opposition?

"It's hard," Franken admits. "It's especially hard with today's social media environment. If you go see a rally for Trump, it's entertaining for an hour or so, simply by nature of how absurd it is. But about 80 percent of what he says is not true. And yet his base absorbs 100 percent of it as reality. It's a very big problem and I don't know how we respond to it other than to put out the truth as effectively as possible . . . but we just don't have the best-informed public. And it's chaotic. It's chaotic."

That chaos, within our wider media ecosystem and our government, isn't a bug, but rather a feature of Bannon's zone-flooding model. And it exclusively benefits Republicans, so—from their perspective—why stop lying? Especially if it comes more naturally for these Republicans to keep themselves in front of cameras in hopes of trending online for saying something ludicrous, inappropriate, and inaccurate. What do you do when the zone starts overflowing after bullshit claims—the insurrectionists were "patriots," vaccinations are killing us, all of Trump's indictments are part of a conspiracy—have already filled the void? What happens once capacity is reached?

Is there any possibility of Americans growing too exhausted from the lunacy and lies to crave hope again? We've learned from the right that rage and grievance can be tapped into as a source of mobilizing voters. That's nothing we should seek to emulate. But people can be reached through their emotional response and by provocative language without the message being mired in rage and racism. We saw, not too long ago, how powerfully Democrats thrived under a clear promise of hope and of change. Crafting a message that resonant is only half the battle. The other half is trusting that your message will be delivered and distributed to the audience that most needs to hear it.

5

MAN BITES DOG

In October 2022, the *New York Times* published a piece headlined "Fears over Fate of Democracy Leave Many Voters Frustrated and Resigned." The subhead: "As democracy frays around them, Republicans and Democrats see different culprits and different risks." The article outlines how those on the left are contending with the dangers posed by the deluge of antidemocratic behavior by the right, from gerrymandering to bans on reproductive rights to election deniers running the government. All very present, very serious threats to democracy . . . and then, this paragraph:

> *Of course, just what is threatening democracy depends on who you talk to. Many Republicans are just as frustrated, convinced that the threat stems from liberal teachers, professors or media personalities who they fear are indoctrinating their children; undocumented immigrants given a path to citizenship; or Democrats widening access to voting so much that they are inviting fraud.*

Because why *wouldn't* we feel as threatened by insurrectionist sympathizers who install a gallows on the National Mall, and refuse to participate in democracy, as we are by liberal schoolteachers pushing a radical agenda of inclusivity? Why shouldn't we resent the immigrants arriving at our borders, hoping that if they work hard enough they might one day become Americans (as my ancestors and presumably yours did).* What will become of us if—*gasp*—too many people exercise their most fundamental right by voting? This article is one of the clearest—albeit, tragically, by no means one of the *only*—examples† of Both Sides journalism, which has enveloped political coverage over the last few decades and contributed to its precipitous loss of public trust over the past several years.

Republicans have never been shy about their desire to change the media landscape. As previously noted, Roger Ailes's 1970 memo served as the foundation for what would eventually become the right-wing media behemoth Fox News. Fox was established in the Clinton era, and its call for the 2000 election was instrumental in handing the presidency to George W. Bush. The formula worked—up to and then through a Republican president inciting an insurrection to retain his grip on power. Far from being left out to dry, Trump received a firehose of on-air support—so much so that Fox ultimately had to pay a record $787.5 million as part of a settlement in a defamation lawsuit brought by Dominion Voting Systems for lies the network knowingly told in Trump's defense. Because he had Ailes's propaganda machine doing its round-the-clock apologia, the outgoing president not only didn't get excommunicated from the party, he continued to lead it.

---

* Should we have Emma Lazarus's words removed from within the Statue of Liberty, and maybe hang a No Vacancy sign around her neck while we're at it?

† That day.

Fox News had ultimately become so openly steeped in shilling for the Republican Party that it shed its "Fair and Balanced" slogan. (Having it in the first place was absurd enough, but actively shedding it really does give the game away, doesn't it?) By 2018, Sean Hannity—who, it was revealed, had regular late-night phone calls with Trump to give the latter an opportunity "to decompress"—freely joined the president onstage at a rally. Fox host Jeanine Pirro was also invited onstage. That's how willing they and their network were to publicly broadcast their partisan allegiance.

All of which should have been enough to immediately and automatically invalidate any suggestion that Fox is a good faith player in the media. But Fox did one thing to ensure its longevity: it presented itself as a counterbalance to the liberal media. And nothing—*nothing!*—could be worse as far as the mainstream media* is concerned than having their nonpartisan, independent, judicious bona fides questioned.

To be clear, this is not to paint the entire media with the same broad brush. There are countless outlets and journalists, hosts, and editors striving to meet the moment with integrity. Their contributions have been invaluable in keeping our democracy afloat. Several of them are featured in this book.

The Trump era has undoubtedly made the job exceedingly difficult. Covering a president who lies more often than he tells the truth, who commands a cultish following, and who craves media validation so desperately that he decorates his global golf clubs with

---

* Widely accepted to mean any media except conservative outlets, even though, let's face it, Fox News alone has more viewers than any other cable network and is about as mainstream as it gets. According to Pew Research, nearly three-quarters of Americans consider Fox part of the mainstream media. But for the purposes of this book, there will be a delineation between conservative media and the rest of the mainstream media.

a fake *Time* magazine cover featuring a full-page photo of his mug has its obvious challenges. Consequently, the distinction between fact and fiction has never been harder to parse, the bad actors seeking to blur those lines have never been more numerous, and the stakes have never felt higher. That makes for immensely challenging work. Those who do it well are nothing less than essential.

My contention is specifically with the Both Sides media, and with outlets that insist on overcompensating so as not to seem liberal. It's with those who offer undue attention to any story presented by the right, as if to prove that it covers both sides in a fair and balanced manner, *and don't you dare call us liberal.*

In doing so, they effectively appoint conservatives as their assignment editors. Not to belabor an overused example, but we saw this most starkly when right-wing media sought to damage Hillary Clinton ahead of the 2016 election. A veritable ocean of ink and airtime was dumped into the investigation of her correspondence. Coverage was coordinated in such a way that her use of a private email server became the only story in every time slot on every conservative outlet. Injury was added to the injustice of it all by the ludicrous claim that this amounted to the greatest national security threat in U.S. history.

It wasn't.

In time, albeit far too late, even Trump's State Department released a report conceding that there was no persuasive evidence of mishandling and that none of the emails on the private server were marked as classified. Of course, the faux outrage continued only until Ivanka Trump, in her role as an advisor to the president, sent hundreds of emails to Cabinet officials and White House aides, often in violation of federal rules. You'll be *shocked* to learn that that story came and went like a fart in a hurricane as far as the media was concerned, making it glaringly obvious that the outrage over Clinton's use of a private server had been manufactured to an appalling degree in a desperate effort to find an excuse to vilify her character and fitness for office.

And yet. Rather than recognizing that this was a coordinated campaign being waged by the Republican Party to destroy the candidacy of the Democratic nominee for president of the United States, much of the mainstream media dutifully took its cues from the right. According to the *Columbia Journalism Review:* "In just six days, *The New York Times* ran as many cover stories about Hillary Clinton's emails as they did about all policy issues combined in the 69 days leading up to the election."

Maybe the *Times* acquiesced to its right-wing assignment editors because it earnestly believed conservatives' allegations against Hillary, or at least wanted to pursue them. Far more likely is the possibility that their motivation wasn't about her at all; it had more to do with making it evident that the outlet was in no way, under no circumstances, biased. In doing so, it offered the umpteenth proof point that it's pretty easy to work the refs if you're a conservative seeking to sway media coverage. The formula is pretty basic: *Make an outrageous claim. Accuse the mainstream media of liberal bias until they cover it. Rinse, repeat.*

I GREW UP AN AVID FAN OF PROFESSIONAL WRESTLING (THEN called the WWF; now called WWE). When I revealed as much, friends would ask, eyebrows raised, *You do know that it's fake, right?* The beauty of professional wrestling, though, is that we fans were all in unspoken agreement to suspend reality in deference to the fantasy that it's not staged, a concept known as "kayfabe." Together, we pretend that an absurd competition that is clearly staged, predetermined, and scripted in fact *isn't,* because the only way it maintains its legitimacy and entertainment value is if we collectively uphold its "reality."

That is what the media is doing with these Republicans.

They know that Republicans are selling them a bill of goods, but the press suspends reality in deference to the greater show and to their ratings. The crucial difference is that instead of the championship belt changing hands from The Rock to Mick Foley, the implications of this iteration of professional wrestling are health care for millions of Americans, the safety of children in schools, and the preservation of our democracy.

Or at least I hope that's what they're doing, because the alternative—that the media actually believes the heaping mounds of daily, verifiable horseshit it's being sold by the GOP—would truly be cause for alarm. As bad as kayfabe sounds, it is leagues preferable to a media that legitimately cannot discern fact from obvious fiction.

Disheartening though it may be, it shouldn't come as a surprise that the mainstream media runs to cover the right's propaganda. Left-wing media gains its "unbiased" legitimacy by criticizing Democrats. Not to be confused with right-wing media, which also gains legitimacy by criticizing Democrats. But though the mainstream media kowtows to the right in hopes of being accepted as legitimate by conservatives . . . they'll never get that acceptance! Conservatives will *still* call the *New York Times* and the *Washington Post* and CNN and the rest of the mainstream media "fake news."*

Regardless, the left should get over this idea that it will ever win over Republicans by doing their editorial bidding or other

---

* Trump claims that he invented the phrase. Fun fact: he didn't. David Bauder, "Fox's Hannity Speaks Onstage at Trump Campaign Rally," Associated Press, November 6, 2018.

displays of goodwill. The left's stories and angles will always be weaponized by the right. What's worse, our media is aware that Republicans are operating in bad faith, considering the effort the GOP has put toward broadcasting as much. They tell on themselves with such shamelessness it's tantamount to taunting. In 2015, during an interview with Sean Hannity, Representative Kevin McCarthy explained, "Everybody thought that Hillary Clinton was unbeatable, right? But we put together a Benghazi Special Committee—a Select Committee. What are her numbers today? Her numbers are dropping." That's right. This guy went on national television and blurted out that the whole point of the Benghazi Select Committee was to hurt Clinton's poll numbers. A two-year, $7 million investigation would ultimately result in an eight-hundred-page report outlining no wrongdoing. Did that stop the media from buying into the narrative that Republicans' outrage over Benghazi was genuine? Not in the slightest.

The GOP has become increasingly transparent about their own crooked motivations. In December 2023, as Republicans were barreling forward with their Biden impeachment inquiry (the evidence for which amounted to three payments of $1,380 each as reimbursement for the purchase of a truck), Representative Troy Nehls was asked what he hoped to gain from the time-consuming, expensive, and nakedly baseless investigation. He replied, "All I can say is Donald J. Trump 2024, baby!"

Given that members of Congress are elected to govern on behalf of their constituents, one might presume that, *Oh, I don't know*, "the truth" or "evidence of high crimes and misdemeanors" might have been more appropriate answers. Instead, Nehls opted to reveal what was patently obvious: that the whole point of moving to impeach Biden was to usher in a Trump presidency, baby.

We've reached the point where Republican lawmakers respond to reporters much as rallygoers wearing LOCK HER UP T-shirts and MAGA hats might. Such officeholders don't hesitate to expose their reasoning even as they acknowledge that their choices and behavior are motivated solely to derive political benefit—and not even for themselves! For Donald Trump! I don't know how many more times Republicans need to bang us over the head with the reality of their intentions for the media to finally believe that they are dealing with bad actors. Whatever that magic number is, we're evidently not there yet.

I'd go so far as to suggest that Republicans have come to rely on the media as allies, even beyond election matters. Remember that whole gamble with our debt ceiling in June 2023 that nearly sent us headlong into recession? Not that I can (or would want to) crawl inside of their minds, but such optics-obsessed Republicans probably wouldn't have been brave enough to risk our own economy unless they felt confident about the way it would be portrayed in the media—and their calculus was correct. Look no further than Bloomberg's piece, "Debt Limit Fight Becomes Fodder for 2024 Attacks by Both Parties." *What?*

The debt ceiling fight was portrayed, incomprehensibly and with no basis in fact, as a *negotiation* between both sides. Business as usual. Run-of-the-mill politicking. It was no such thing. This was the Republicans threatening to blow up, in midair, the plane we were all on. Any rational coverage would be clear-eyed about the fact that the GOP was looking to use the threat of default—meaning economic collapse—to exact unpopular political concessions. Key word: rational.

So why did the Republicans feel so comfortable flirting with the demise of our financial system—a financial system in which they take part? Partially because they knew it would be written about in such a way that would cover their asses. But also because they had the luxury of confidence. They knew that the Democrats wouldn't let default happen: Democrats are responsible enough not to want to usher in financial ruin; they are *actually* fiscally responsible. So, taking advantage of the fact that Democrats wouldn't let our economy fail, Republicans implemented as pernicious a scheme as they could cook up. Speaker McCarthy—for the hottest of seconds the government's highest-ranking Republican—was asked what he was willing to give up in the "negotiations." His response was that he would lift the debt ceiling. His *concession* was that he would avoid making the domestic and global economies crash. How's that for compromise?

It's especially perplexing that, as Republicans threaten to crash the plane we're all on (whether with regard to the economy or democracy itself), the press is *also on the plane*. If the plane goes down, we all die. They've got skin in the game, too. Which is among the reasons why, at a bare minimum, yes, "the media in this country should have a bias—in favor of democracy," Mehdi Hasan explained, "because democracy is what we depend on to survive." Without it, there wouldn't be a free press, so it seems counterintuitive for the media to continue on the path of Both Sides-ing *itself* into obscurity.

"Legacy media has this debate where we need to present all arguments, because that's our role," Jen Psaki explained. "Okay . . . but we're also in an existential moment right now, and isn't speaking out about that existential moment also part of the role?" Even for a media obsessed with balance, defending democracy should come first; that should be the foundation on which the rest of the coverage is built, not the other way around.

ONE MEDIA-MANIPULATION STRATEGY THAT PROVED ESPECIALLY effective for Trump was creating the curve on which he would ultimately be graded. "The example I always give," Hasan offered, "is Viscount Northcliffe, who was the famous British newspaper baron who owned the *Daily Mail* and the *Daily Mirror* and the *Times* of London at the turn of the twentieth century. He's the guy who allegedly said, 'Dog bites man is not journalism because it happens so often. Man bites dog is news, right?' The key phrase . . . is 'because it happens so often.' The reason why man bites dog *is* news is because, 'wow, a man bit a dog.' Trump has done stuff that is 'whoa, man bites dog,' but *because it happens so often*, it becomes not news.

"In any other scenario, in any other country, in any other political system, with any other politician who was indicted, who was found liable of sexual assault in court, who incited an insurrection, threatened members of the public, threatened the media, etc., etc., those would all be huge stories and would all be 'man bites dog' stories. Trump has broken that model by simply, to quote Steve Bannon, flooding the zone and normalizing this shit. By Gish galloping,"* Hasan explained. "He just doesn't fit within our normal ways of coverage, because he's overloaded us with shit."

I'm not here to credit Trump for masterminding an entirely new strategy, although he certainly is the first president to roll it out as a daily media tactic, whether consciously or because he has no filter. What is almost more impressive† is that, as far as the media is

---

* A term he covered extensively in his own book that essentially means burying your opponent with so many obfuscations that they can't possibly rebut them all.

† Insofar as the worst person doing something so deeply destructive could be regarded or referred to as "impressive."

concerned, this allowance is only afforded to Republicans. The GOP has leapt on the Trump train and, perhaps brilliantly, managed to lower the public's confidence so much that any expectation for them to behave as full participants in democracy has all but vanished.

"Why is it that the media *only* holds the Democrats to any kind of standard?" Hasan asked. "The Republicans get a pass! All of the coverage is based around the Democrats being held to certain standards, the Democrats following certain rules. The Republicans? Well, of course they're not going to follow them. And we've accepted and priced that into the conversation: that Republicans can't be held responsible for anything. That's why all of the coverage about deals and compromise asks, 'Where's Biden? Where are the Democrats? The Republicans? Oh, they're not going to accept it, of course.' Was I away the day we all agreed that Republicans would not be held to any standards when it comes to government shutdowns or immigration compromises or Speaker votes? It's not even both sides, it really is only one-side-ism."

Mainstream media journalists are now aware of this imbalance, but they've simply allowed Republicans to be graded on a curve. They've gotten used to men biting dogs. They've gotten used to the shameless politicking, the hostage-taking, the threats, the violence, and the lies from the right. That's become the new baseline for Republicans. And because those members of the media have come to expect so very little out of the party, the Republicans have managed to evade accountability for consistently failing to do their jobs.

Take the most obvious and abhorrent example imaginable: when the former president and presumed Republican nominee echoed the language of Adolf Hitler by accusing immigrants* of

---

* For posterity, that would include two of his three wives—the mothers of four of his five known children.

"poisoning the blood of our country," the media shrugged—in part because, after all, he's already done that. That dog's been bitten. It's not fresh or exciting or newsworthy the second time, let alone the third, fourth, or fifteenth time. Furthermore, by the time Trump's Hitleresque invocation of the blood of the country made its way through the normalizing machine of our media, we were left with headlines and justifications like these:

CBS NEWS ANALYSIS: *Most Republicans agree with "poisoning the blood" language. "A striking number of voters agree with this description of immigrants who enter the U.S. illegally, and among Republicans, associating the remarks with Trump himself makes them even likelier to agree."*

ROLL CALL: *Tuberville backs Trump's "poisoning the blood" rhetoric. "'I'm mad he wasn't even tougher than that,' Alabama Republican says."*

THE HILL: *Johnson defends Trump's "poisoning" immigrant remark. "Well, it's not hateful," Johnson said. "What President Trump is trying to advance is his America first priority. And I think that makes sense to a lot of people. . . . President Biden wants additional supplemental spending on national security, but he denies the most important point of our own national security. And that is our own border."*

Imagine being given the opportunity to either breathlessly condemn Hitleresque rhetoric or twist yourself into knots to defend it . . . *and opting to do the latter!*

Republicans have mastered the art of continuously shifting the Overton window wherein they'll push the envelope so much that what seemed insane five minutes ago now seems banal by comparison. Doing as much is a means of giving themselves permission to be as extreme as they'd like. And it doesn't get more extreme than echoing Adolf Hitler; nor does it get more unacceptable than the press framing such language through the exact same filter as it uses for every other story.

As if the example of Hitler is somehow not enough to prove this point,* another salient example of the GOP gaming the refs is evidenced in the coverage of Joe Biden's age, which in the lead-up to the 2024 election became his biggest political liability. Biden is in fact our oldest president. He has never been an especially eloquent orator (he famously overcame a stutter). It was not surprising, then, for the right to brand him as being in the throes of cognitive decline and suggest that he's not up for another term.

But rather than acknowledge that Biden has already disproved the notion of senility by *doing* the job (and accomplishing more than any president in modern U.S. history, I should add), the media glommed on to this narrative, taking the Republicans' attacks at face value and oversaturating their coverage with constant references to *Joe Biden's age problem.* Which in turn has created media cycles about his age, which was reflected in polling, which spurred more coverage, reflected in yet more polling. On and on the vicious cycle continued. The issue of Biden's age was birthed by the GOP but raised by its willful accomplices in the media.

We became inundated with articles, television coverage, posts, and headlines questioning whether the guy who added the greatest number of jobs in U.S. history might be up for the job. Whether the guy who presided over the longest stretch of sub–4 percent unemployment in the last half century might be up for the job.

---

* It is.

Whether the guy who led the U.S. to the fastest economic recovery of all modernized countries in the aftermath of a bruising global pandemic might be up for the job. Whether the guy who turned the Trump-era punch line of upgrading our nation's infrastructure into a reality; who delivered on the first gun safety legislation in three decades; who got the government to negotiate lower drug prices and got insulin manufacturers to slash their costs 65 to 80 percent and delivered record climate action might be up for the job. To be clear, none of this is to suggest that Joe Biden is perfect or that we aren't entitled to worry about having an octogenarian commander in chief; it's merely to impart the absurdity of this blanket refusal to evaluate, while wondering if Biden *could* be president, his success *at* being president.

Still, despite his obvious proven effectiveness, the media took its cues from its assignment editors on the right. CNN hosted a round-table discussion panel with the chyron: *IS BIDEN'S AGE NOW A BIGGER PROBLEM THAN TRUMP'S INDICTMENTS?* The *New York Times* published a piece under the headline "Which Is Worse: Biden's Age or Trump Handing NATO to Putin?" CNN published one headlined "The 2024 Campaign Gets Grimmer, with Trump's Extremism on Full Display Alongside Concerns over Biden's Age."

Presumably these authors and hosts know that Joe Biden simply being old is not a "bigger problem" or "worse" than the prospect of a man who's contending with eighty-eight criminal charges turning the Department of Justice into his personal fiefdom. Presumably they know that Joe Biden's age is not, in fact, worse than Trump dismantling the alliance responsible for upholding the postwar global order and preserving peace in the aftermath of two world wars. Presumably they know that Joe Biden's age is not worse than Donald Trump's extremism, which includes promises to deploy the U.S. military to Democratic cities and carry out the "largest domestic deportation operation in American history." But still they pose the question, knowing that the net effect of doing so will be the perpetuation of these perilous ideas. For as much as Tucker Carlson is probably despised by mainstream media figures, these headlines and chyrons are not dissimilar to his "just asking questions" shtick. He knows that what he's saying is bullshit, but because he frames that bullshit as an innocent question rather than a certainty, he gets his point across while still giving himself just enough padding to maintain plausible deniability.

While the media is busy trying to bury Joe Biden, Trump enjoys a free pass despite the hot garbage that he spews on a near-daily basis. In a normal world, that garbage would *actually justify* so breezily aiming "cognitive decline" headlines at Trump. Here's a small sampling of the hypotheses, suggestions, and claims made by Donald Trump leading up to the 2024 election: that Barack Obama was the current president; that Jeb Bush got the United States involved in wars in the Middle East; that World War II hasn't happened yet; that he won all fifty states in 2020 (including California); that "U.S." (as in United States) also spells the word "us," and that he may have been the first person in history to make that connection; that Viktor Orbán was the leader of Turkey (that would be Erdogan); that you need ID to buy bread; that water destroys magnets; and that Nikki Haley was in charge of security at the U.S. Capitol on January 6. Joe Biden could misplace a modifier in a sentence and Fox News would line up a panel of neurologists frothing to diagnose his cognitive impairment, but Donald Trump confuses his own Republican UN ambassador with the Democratic Speaker of the House on multiple occasions and it's accepted as a totally normal whoopsies.

We could also play the most revealing game in politics: *Imagine* *if Barack Obama did that.* What would the coverage on Fox look like if Barack Obama got indicted? What if Obama was charged on eighty-eight criminal counts? What if Obama stole classified documents from the White House but justified his actions by claiming that he'd already declassified everything with his mind? What if Obama tried to extort a foreign leader by withholding military assistance for dirt on Donald Trump? What if Obama called members of the military "suckers" and "losers"? What if Obama invited the Taliban to Camp David on the anniversary of September 11? I could go on and on and on,* but the answer to those questions is always the same: far from being ignored by

---

* What if Obama suggested injecting disinfectant as a cure for COVID? What if Obama openly mocked a disabled reporter? What if Obama lost 2.9 million jobs during his presidency while hailing himself the *jobs jobs jobs president*? What if Obama's first national security advisor resigned within one month for lying to the FBI about interactions with Russia's ambassador? What if Obama refused to divest from his international business organizations? What if Obama paid off a known porn star for her silence about their affair? What if Obama's campaign manager was found guilty of tax and bank fraud and later pleaded guilty to money laundering, tax evasion, and witness tampering? What if Obama sent regular after-midnight tweets addressing "negative press covfefe"? What if Obama encouraged his supporters to engage in physical violence at his rallies? What if Obama refused to condemn neo-Nazis? What if Obama proudly compared his coronavirus press briefings, intended to inform a terrified public about how to survive, to a Mike Tyson boxing match? What if Obama used emergency authority to circumvent Congress on a border wall that was never built? What if Obama crudely disparaged opponents and proposed the execution of a respected military leader? What if Obama regularly flattered Vladimir Putin and other global dictators? What if Obama visited one of our territories after a devastating hurricane, complained that it was costing him too much money, then showed his empathy by throwing rolls of paper towels at victims of the disaster as though he were participating in a half-time show stunt? What if Obama congratulated China on the anniversary of its Communist takeover? What if Obama discussed imposing martial law at an Oval Office meeting? What if Obama pardoned a number of war criminals? What if Obama demanded personal loyalty over fulfilling one's constitutional oath? What if Obama called immigrants vermin? What if Obama was found liable of sexual assault and defamation for cornering a woman in the dressing room of a department store? What if Obama refused to commit to a peaceful transfer of power . . . and, for once, kept his word? What if Obama incited rioters to enter the Capitol and launched an insurrection? What if Obama then told those insurrectionists "we love you" and called them patriots? What if Obama used campaign finances to pay his not insubstantial legal bills? What if Obama said he would "encourage" Russia "to do whatever the hell they want" to countries that are part of NATO? What if Obama confirmed that, if elected, he would become a dictator for a day? What if . . . well, I think you get it.

right-wing media, it would be treated as the five-alarm fire that this abhorrent pattern of behavior actually merits.

The asymmetry of standards is so obvious that Obama himself drew attention to it. "We know that he [Trump] continues to do business with China because he's got a secret Chinese bank account," Obama said incredulously while on the stump for Biden in late 2020. "How is that possible? A secret Chinese bank account. Listen, can you imagine if I'd had a secret Chinese bank account when I was running for reelection? You think Fox News might've been a little concerned about that? They would've called me Beijing Barry."

In fact, you don't have to take my word for it. Nor do we need to engage in hypotheticals: we have the luxury* of an apples-to-apples comparison. Jim Jordan, an elected representative, flouted a congressional subpoena issued by the January 6 Committee to testify about his role in Republican efforts to undermine the 2020 election results. Right-wing media ignored it.

But when Hunter Biden, a private citizen, initially refused to testify in a private deposition as part of the Oversight Committee's evidence-free impeachment inquiry into Joe Biden, knowing full well that any private testimony would ultimately be distorted by the committee's Republican members, many of whom lie as easily as the sun rises in the morning, right-wing media treated his snub as if it were their very own Pearl Harbor.

Fox News ran the headline: "Hunter Biden Faces Backlash After Defying Subpoena with Press Conference 'Stunt': 'Hold Him in Contempt!'" And Jim Jordan sought to do exactly that, approving a contempt resolution against Hunter. The fact that Jordan, himself *still in violation* of a congressional subpoena,

---

* Grave misfortune.

would seek to hold Hunter Biden in contempt of Congress for refusing to comply with a congressional subpoena only adds to the steaming pile of proof that shame and standards are no longer a consideration of the right.

THE QUESTION WE SO OFTEN WRESTLE WITH, AS CITIZENS generally aware of the role the press played in getting Trump elected in 2016, is: Has the media learned its lesson? When I asked Hasan that question, he directed my attention to the headline and subhead from that very day's *New York Times*:

HOW BIDEN'S IMMIGRATION FIGHT THREATENS HIS BIGGEST FOREIGN POLICY WIN

The debate over immigration in the United States is spilling over into other parts of President Biden's agenda, particularly the war in Ukraine.

The reality of President Biden's "immigration fight" on the day that headline was posted, January 19, 2024, is that, after years (read: decades) of Republicans wailing about the border, they finally found a willing negotiating partner in Joe Biden, who sought to strike a deal. *Surely* the GOP would leap at the opportunity to solve a problem as serious and urgent and dangerous as the border. After all, the border had been the subject of an ongoing and indefatigable fear campaign about terrorists and drugs and fentanyl and rapists.

Finally the Republicans had the opportunity to fix it *and* score a massively conservative deal. The bipartisan plan that Biden ultimately endorsed would impose tight restrictions on the border *without* comprehensive immigration reform—a coup for Republicans (not quite the coup they were hoping for, but a coup nonetheless).

Like clockwork, Trump issued his clarion call on Truth Social: "A Border Deal now would be another Gift to the Radical Left Democrats. They need it politically, but don't care about our Border." In other words, he was cooing a signal to his henchmen and hangers-on in Congress that striking a deal and resolving the issue would be politically advantageous for Joe Biden and the Democrats. He would rather have the issue remain unresolved, so that he has something to run on and some way to deflect any questions that might be pointed at, *oh, I don't know*, his excess of criminal charges, perhaps?

Trump's sycophants heard the call and sprang into action— well, inaction. "Let me tell you, I'm not willing to do too damn much right now to help a Democrat and to help Joe Biden's approval rating," said Republican representative Troy Nehls of Texas, whose every public comment seems further evidence of his sad, shameless subservience to Donald Trump. "I will not help the Democrats try to improve this man's dismal approval ratings. I'm not going to do it. Why would I?" I don't know, Troy. Maybe because your party has spent years asking for precisely what Biden just offered?

And then there's Mike Johnson, who, upon being elected Speaker of the House, gave himself goose bumps when he said, "We must come together and address the broken border." However, he didn't mean that they should come together. Nor did he have any intention of addressing the broken border. Instead, as soon as he heard the marching orders from Trump, he called any potential deal "dead on arrival in the House."

Everyone's least favorite sprinter in the Senate, Josh Hawley, said, "There is absolutely no reason to agree to policies that will just further enable Joe Biden." McConnell, Senate minority leader, joined the choir, and was quoted as saying, "We don't want to do anything to undermine him," referencing Trump. Senator Ted Cruz, who only months earlier had introduced the Secure the Border Act, suddenly decided, "We don't need a border bill." Fox host Shannon Bream, who had no business joining this conversation but has evidently drawn inspiration from this troop of sycophants, grilled Senator James Lankford, the conservative Republican who had worked to craft this doomed bipartisan border deal, on the prospect of helping Biden secure a win. "Why give him this?" she asked, pointing out that doing so would mean that Biden "gets to take a victory lap that he's gotten something done." The horror!

And in case all of that was too subtle, Lankford himself stood on the Senate floor and admitted, "I had a popular commentator four weeks ago that I talked to, that told me flat out—before they knew any of the contents of the bill, nothing was out at that point—he told me flat out, 'If you try to move a bill that solves the border crisis during this presidential year, I will do whatever I can to destroy you. Because I do not want you to solve this during the presidential election.' By the way, they have been faithful to their promise and have done everything they can to destroy me."

That is the harsh reality of Biden's "immigration fight." One side—the Democrats—extended themselves in service of solving a problem. The other side—the Republicans—not only weren't willing to sacrifice the *issue* of the border but went so far as to publicly broadcast their strategy and corrupt rationale! Despite their brazen transparency, what the public received was a headline decrying some nebulous immigration fight, devoid of any antagonists whatsoever, as if the whole thing had occurred in a vacuum.

"Now *that* is a classic example," Hasan said, referring again to that day's headline.* "What is missing from there? Any mention of the Republican Party, which are the people blocking the deal! Not only blocking the deal, but *shamelessly* saying, 'Why would we give him a deal? That would help him in the election?' Mike Johnson is openly saying this; Troy Nehls is openly saying this. But instead of the headline being 'Republicans Block Immigration Compromise on Behalf of Donald Trump,' the headline becomes about Biden, while the GOP is erased. That, for me, is the prime evidence on the day you're asking me the question 'Have we learned anything?'" The answer, according to Hasan, is no.

Now, there's a tendency among liberals to throw their hands up and decry how *unfair* all of this is. What about justice? What about a level playing field? What about the rules? We're going up against a fundamentally antidemocratic opposition, propped up by a right-wing disinformation machine that is further enabled by a mainstream media apparatus unwilling and unable to meet the moment.

So, no, it is not fair. But the time has come to disabuse ourselves of the notion that the fourth estate is going to rescue us, inform us fairly, or even be a partner in democracy. Democrats need to stop clinging to this romanticized idea of what the media is—that it's still Bob Woodard and Carl Bernstein; still a glossy Hollywood story about the good guys swooping in to save us by delivering the truth to newsstands across the nation. If it was 2016, that would be one thing, and we could certainly be forgiven for believing in a

---

* "How Biden's Immigration Fight Threatens His Biggest Foreign Policy Win."

fair press. But go back to the example Hasan offered from 2024, or maybe scroll through today's paper. We're still contending with the same tired Both Sides-ism almost a decade after Trump first cannonballed onto the scene. These failures of coverage can no longer be viewed as a fluke; they are a pattern. They are not going to change. If we can watch nearly a decade pass us by with the media still largely broken and tilted, then guess what: it is going to stay broken. More dispiriting than the failures of the press is our inability to recognize that this is not going to change. But most dispiriting of all is our unwillingness to do something about it.

So let's do something about it.

6

IF YOU BUILD IT . . .

Republicans of another era had the foresight and discipline to create their own media distribution system, with a long-term vision. It would be effective at reaching its intended base, and it would deliver content catered to the party and its supporters. The machine goes as far back as the mid-1960s, when Richard Viguerie—sometimes known as the "funding father of the conservative movement"—started doing an end run around traditional media by using direct mail and building up extensive lists (with an estimated 3.5 million names) of conservative supporters. Many of those on the lists would become donors to the cause. Over the decades, his company has sent more than two billion letters, with the aim to, according to the *Washington Post*, "build support for 'New Right' causes that range from cutting taxes to bolstering family values."

When Lewis Powell shared his influential memo with corporate America, he knew that success would hinge on discipline and collective persistence. "Strength lies in organization," he wrote, "in careful long-range planning and implementation, in consistency of action over an indefinite period of years, in the scale of financing available only through joint effort, and in the political power available only through united action and national organizations."

The Fairness Doctrine had come into play about a decade and a half prior, provoked by lawmakers concerned that the three main television networks—NBC, ABC, and CBS—had a monopoly on the press and could use it to set a biased public agenda. It mandated that the networks give time to contrasting views on issues of public importance. Congress gradually built up support for the doctrine, and the Federal Communications Commission (FCC) called it the "single most important requirement of operation in the public interest." The doctrine kept broadcasters from presenting the news from a single point of view, was upheld in the Supreme Court, and remained in place until the Reagan administration. In 1985, the FCC under Mark Fowler asserted that it was in fact not in the public interest, and that enforcement violated the First Amendment.

The doctrine was rolled back during Reagan's second term, despite complaints that it was the only guardrail that would prevent broadcast journalists, if left unchecked, from verbally assaulting politicians and their policies on-air—paving the road for the likes of Limbaugh. It was repealed by the FCC on August 5, 1987. Members of Congress opposed the decision, with South Carolina Democrat Ernest F. Hollings arguing that it was "wrongheaded, misguided, and illogical." Earlier in the year, Congress had attempted to codify the Fairness Doctrine in new legislation, the Fairness in Broadcasting Act, which had passed, only to be vetoed by President Reagan in June.

Reagan's intervention would give a wide berth and that much more freedom to, among others, Limbaugh, the grand wizard of making the airwaves partisan while spreading unchecked lies and leaning way, way into his own bias and agenda, both of which targeted liberals as the enemy. Limbaugh, not known for his humility, said of his show: "This has not been an AM-radio revolution exclusively; it has been a conservative-media revolution." Of his content, he said, with characteristic candor and lack of grace: "I made fun of liberals, espoused and explained conservatism, and promoted traditional American values. And audiences ate it up; they had been starved for it."

Reagan once called Limbaugh "the Number One voice for conservatism in our Country."

That number one voice of U.S. conservatism wrote or offered commentary such as:

Feminism was established so as to allow unattractive women access to the mainstream of society.

I think it's time to get rid of this whole National Basketball Association. Call it the TBA, the Thug Basketball Association, and stop calling them teams. Call 'em gangs.

If any race of people should not have guilt about slavery, it's Caucasians. The white race has probably had fewer slaves, and for a briefer period of time, than any other in the history of the world.

When a gay person turns his back on you, it is anything but an insult; it's an invitation.

In 2007, when Obama was in the Senate and gaining popularity, Limbaugh began airing a song called "Barack, the Magic Negro."

And so, of course, Trump awarded Limbaugh the Presidential Medal of Freedom.

The day after the 2021 inauguration, Limbaugh repeatedly said on-air that Biden had not won the election—and dismissed the pro-Trump mob that had stormed the U.S. Capitol.

ON TO THE SCREEN. WE SAW HOW ROGER AILES AND CABLE NEWS (with the creation of outlets like Fox, Newsmax, and OANN) built a protective shield around the information being delivered to audiences. This way, conservative leaders got the benefit of the doubt, while pesky matters such as "facts" and "reality" ceased becoming an obstacle to airing the right's version of the truth.

Today the internet provides massive silos of Republican disinformation through targeted "news" shows and websites: Breitbart, the Daily Wire, the Daily Caller, Steve Bannon's *War Room*, Alex Jones's *Infowars*. Which is to say nothing of the far-right extremist sites that cater to conservatives, conspiracy theorists, and the disenfranchised. Vulnerable audiences are targeted with surgical precision. And political knowledge and biases are formed and deemed accurate without the help of fact. Angry, uninformed bloggers with an agenda of hatred and vitriol are given free rein to offer the news.

The MAGA movement revved to life within this environment. As Hasan said, "You can't understand the Trump phenomenon unless you understand the role that independent media on the right has played in terms of social media, in terms of amplification of his message, in terms of getting his fake news across."

At one point, Trump's Twitter and Facebook accounts had more than 88.8 million and close to 35 million followers, respectively. And when he was kicked off both platforms, a growing body of neo-Nazis and conspiracy theorists were there to fill his dangerous, rage-filled void.

In 2023, Trump invited several of these right-wing influencers to dine with him at Mar-a-Lago. The guest list included Jack Posobiec, of Pizzagate notoriety; Chaya Raichik, curator of the far right, anti-LGBTQ+ hate machine Libs of TikTok; Rogan O'Handley, known as DC Draino; Newsmax producer Alex Lorusso; and other young fury-generators. One can only imagine (though I apologize for suggesting you even do that) the raucous hate shared around the table. Apparently Trump was informed that it was important to court these adoring guests—so, according to the Daily Beast, no expense was spared: his digital mouthpieces were treated to the finest cheeseburgers, jumbo shrimp, and Diet Coke his donors' money could buy.

From direct mailing to detailed memos of how to create a coalition to prolific online forums and rising spokespeople, the cogs of the right-wing media infrastructure have been manufactured into place over the course of more than half a century with military-style organization. We like to think that *Elizabeth Warren* had plans? Warren's comprehensive strategies were fleeting ideas thrown into the wind compared with the long-term projects laid out and executed by the de facto founders of the conservative media movement: Viguerie and Powell, Limbaugh and Ailes, Gingrich* and Bannon.

The Republican Party continues to enjoy a full-scale propaganda machine, one which insulates its followers in a hermetically sealed bubble, free from the risks posed by, well, the truth. Trump has taken advantage of these channels, amplified many of them, and—going a step further—exploited them. Ironically, he used the

---

* Though Gingrich was a member of Congress, and Powell an attorney then a Supreme Court justice, both were acutely aware of (and specific about) how to use media to achieve their party's goals.

machine to such an extent that he effectively chipped away at the Republicans' facade and left it exposed. As Rush Limbaugh said in 2016, assessing Trump's coalition of radicals, "It is everything that the Republican Party claims they want, and they don't want it with Trump in charge of it."

Of course they don't want Trump in charge. His controversial, inappropriate, ungodly, immoral, hysterical, un-American, anti-democratic, deranged rhetoric stirred up and illuminated all the dysfunction that the GOP has basically trademarked. But even they couldn't have known the black holes he would lead the party into—from the moment they handed him one of their gilded megaphones. He grasped hold of it, ripped the filter out, began shrieking lies about how many people had attended his inauguration, and has yet to cede control of that megaphone since.*

He has exposed those who have endorsed his behavior and out-landish statements—none of which reflect traditional Republican values, traditional Christian values, or any sort of moral high ground—as being complete frauds. All the words and labels they've safely hidden behind for decades? Donald Trump has rendered all of them meaningless. He has been the great unmasker of the Republican Party, taking their professed values and proving to the world that they were baseless talking points that don't mean a damn thing.

And yet the conservative media machine is still running. Which prompts the obvious question: Why haven't Democrats, who are still passing legislation and whose values are relatively intact, offered a counterpoint?

"The problem in my mind," explained Dan Pfeiffer, "is that 95 percent of the energy in the party and in the people who are

---

* One can only assume it's beside reams of classified documents in one of his bathrooms in Mar-a-Lago.

dedicating intellectual capital to messaging spend it on what the message is, not how to get people to hear it. Because of the multiple channels and media systems Republicans have built up, they are just better at delivering their message in front of people than we are. So we have a much bigger message *distribution* problem than a message *conception* problem."

It's not to say messaging isn't important; working toward a lucid bumper sticker (a *singular* bumper sticker, to Franken's point) matters. But what good is a slogan if no one hears it? "You need a full soup-to-nuts strategy to actually get your message out," Pfeiffer said. "Even if you pick up the perfect message but are just delivering it through the old ways of doing it, it's the existential tree falling in the forest situation."

The need for that soup-to-nuts strategy is apparent not just from a distribution perspective but also from a financial one. Stephanie Valencia, cofounder of the Latino Media Network, explained on an episode of *Pod Save America* in July 2021: "Republicans just bought this conservative-backed media entity, one of the last, more neutral radio stations in South Florida, for three hundred fifty thousand dollars. *Three hundred fifty thousand dollars!* Some Democratic donors can find that as pocket change in their couch. Meanwhile, Democrats spent fourteen million dollars in the last thirty days in the South Florida media market alone. Literally setting money on fire with paid media that probably nobody remembers. And now Republicans are going to have yet another tool and weapon in their arsenal to reach and engage and persuade Latino voters."

For all their good intentions, Democrats have yet to create a strategy that comes anywhere near rivaling the right-wing media ecosystem. "Democrats spend all this time in campaigns doing polls, research, fine-tuning to get the perfect message that we believe to our core will persuade the voters we need," said Pfeiffer.

"Then we hand that message to CNN or the *New York Times* and say, 'Please deliver it to them.' Then they put it in their own packaging and they put it through a horse race filter. It is not their job to elect Democrats, for sure, but therefore it also makes them a terrible vehicle to distribute our information."

Which gives Republicans a clear, unearned advantage, given that even the slowest guy on earth is bound to win a race if he's the only one running.

Why are Democrats unpersuaded by this? Why do they remain obstinate in their belief that the ideal message delivery system is the mainstream media? The mainstream media has broadcast (literally and figuratively) that it is not on Democrats' side; why insist, then, that this is the best they've got?

It doesn't have to be that way.

It's impossible to see the success that the right has had within its own independent media ecosystem and to still pretend that relying on traditional outlets like the *Washington Post* is any kind of solution. Among the *Post*'s headlines and subheads early in 2024:

AMERICANS KNOW TRUMP IS EXTREME. THEY MIGHT ELECT HIM ANYWAY

Yes, Americans think Trump will do those drastic things. They don't necessarily view them as disqualifying.

Republicans Now Say It Might Be Okay to Ignore the Supreme Court

That's the liberal media? That's the coverage that represents and advocates for our interests?

Or is it the *New York Times*, which frames fringe Republicans getting saved over debt ceiling agreements as a compromise between equal counterparts: "With both far-right and hard-left lawmakers in revolt over the deal, it fell to a bipartisan coalition powered by Democrats to push the bill over the finish line, throwing their support behind the compromise in an effort to break the fiscal stalemate that had gripped Washington for weeks." Is *that* what qualifies as the liberal media?

Putting aside what a gross disservice it is to even propose that those two options are in any way equivalent (the far right includes nihilists and election deniers like Lauren Boebert and anime enthusiast Paul Gosar, while the "hard left" includes progressives like Bernie Sanders and AOC, whose most "radical" proposal is health care for everyone), we need to stop denying a very obvious conclusion: our supposedly liberal media is not actually a liberal media.

We cannot sit by and idly accept, say, Chris Christie on some ABC News panel offering mild pushback against Donald Trump (whose rise to power *he aided*). His is a voice that represents really *no one's* interests. We have to demand more than the crumbs we're being given. Better yet, we have to start baking our own bread. Witnessing daily examples of this Both Sides nonsense and growing complacent about it is bad enough. To then compare it with the well-oiled propaganda machine on the right, and to continue wondering why Democrats are constantly put on the defensive, makes our refusal to invest in a distribution system of our own tantamount to malpractice.

Republicans have enjoyed success in spite of the fact that their message and messengers are horrendous. "Every political activist, every donor, every person who talks about politics, has this sense that the Republicans are great at messaging," Pfeiffer says. "Every donor asks, *Why are Republicans so good on TV?* Watch the Republicans on TV. They suck. They are terrible.

"Mitch McConnell has been the leader of the Senate Republicans for sixteen years. He is one of the worst messengers in American history. Kevin McCarthy? Terrible messenger. Mike Johnson? Super awkward. Ron DeSantis? Awful. Nikki Haley? Barely passable. Donald Trump, who is a master of getting attention, says insane things all the time and constantly steps on his own message. Marjorie Taylor Greene, Lauren Boebert, Nancy Mace, all of these people are terrible!"

I've been closely watching these Republicans for the better part of the last eight years. First of all, someone give me back those eight years. But second, Dan is right. The myths surrounding Republicans—their strengths, what they stand for, their branding savvy—all of that has persisted in spite of regular evidence suggesting otherwise.

While they might be* terrible, they have that latitude because they're being propped up by a media ecosystem designed to never let them fall. In March 2023, Sean Hannity interviewed Donald Trump in an attempt to massage his blatant theft and illegal retention of classified documents from the White House.

HANNITY: *I can't imagine you ever saying: "Bring me some of the boxes that we brought back from the White House. I'd like to look at them." Did you ever do that?*

TRUMP: *I would have the right to do that. There's nothing wrong with it.*

HANNITY: *But I know you. I don't think you would do it.*

---

* are

TRUMP: *Well, I don't have a lot of time. But I would have the right to do that. I would do that. There would be nothing wrong.*

It was clear at this point that Trump was not grabbing hold of the life preserver being shoved in his face, so Hannity tried to cut the boss's losses:

HANNITY: *All right, let me move on—*

But Trump wasn't done digging his hole yet. To the dismay of Hannity, Fox News, and his own criminal attorneys, he continued:

TRUMP: *Remember this: this is the Presidential Records Act. I have the right to take stuff . . . I have the right to take stuff. I have the right to look at stuff.*

Not only did Trump admit to the theft of those classified documents, he also satisfied the question of intent. He was aware of what he possessed and yet maintained that he would "have the right" to keep it (in fact, he absolutely does not have the right to keep boxes of classified documents at his beach resort or golf club/ex-wife's burial grounds). Hannity placed Trump on third base so that he could steal home; instead Trump wandered off the field and into the parking lot because he thought he heard people chanting his name.

Hannity also hosted a televised town hall with Trump in December 2023. In an effort to allow Trump to assuage concerns raised by his promise of retribution, the Fox host lobbed his pal a softball: "To be clear, do you in any way have any plans whatsoever if reelected president to abuse power, to break the law, to use the government to go after people?" Trump deflected: "You mean like they're using right now?"

For the record, Donald, the correct answer was *no*.

And even though Hannity walked that horse right to the water and pointed to the water and splashed it around and cupped some water in his hands and lifted them up to Trump's lips, still he refused to drink. Given every possible cue, Trump managed to bungle the response.*

But because Fox's priority is to abide by some twisted version of the Hippocratic oath with Republicans and first do no harm, Hannity gave Trump a second chance during that same town hall. This time, he would be even clearer and more direct, doing everything he could to allay any anxiety that Trump's initial non-answer might have caused. "The media has been focused on this and attacking you," Hannity began, speaking slowly and deliberately, with a tone generally reserved for explaining basic concepts to a toddler. "Under no circumstances, you are promising America tonight, you would never abuse power as retribution against anybody?" All he needed was a simple *yes* and they could finally move on. That's . . . not what he got. What he got was the declaration already mentioned, but worth repeating, lest anybody forget what Trump's vision for the future of our country actually looks like.

TRUMP: *Except for day one.*

HANNITY: *Except for—*

TRUMP: *Look, he's going crazy. Except for day one.*

---

* I will remind you of Dan's words: "Watch the Republicans on TV. They suck. They are terrible."

HANNITY: *Meaning?*

TRUMP: *I want to close the border and I want to drill—*

HANNITY: *That's not—*

TRUMP: *—drill—*

HANNITY: *That's not—*

TRUMP: *—drill—*

HANNITY: *That's not retribution.*

TRUMP: *We love this guy. He says, "You're not going to be a dictator, are you?" I said: "No, no, no, other than day one."*

Hannity, desperate to clean up Trump's mess, was basically falling out of his seat to insist that Trump's self-proclaimed dictatorial activities didn't *really* qualify as dictatorial, all in an effort to salvage what even he knew was a disastrous moment. Again, Trump didn't have to do anything; Hannity had teed him up perfectly. And yet still Trump couldn't help but insist that he would be a dictator for one day (which assuaged all concerns, because, as we all know, dictators famously abide by self-imposed limits on their own power). In fact, by going so far as to mock Hannity for his efforts, Trump gave the whole game away—exposing Hannity for trying to help him *and* acknowledging that he was unwilling to be helped.*

---

* Again: "Watch the Republicans on TV. They suck. They are terrible."

SOME PROGRESS HAS BEEN MADE WITHIN THE DEMOCRATIC
Party. It can be seen in the increasing numbers of politicians who
have come to understand the necessity of nurturing a progressive
or independent media ecosystem. And yet "not enough people
are doing it," Pfeiffer contends. "Part of that is generational.
Politicians are often frozen in amber in the media environment in
which they rose to power."

But it's not exclusively a generational problem, and the fossil-
ization of past ideals extends beyond the media. Even relatively
young Democrats seem willfully stuck in the mindset that this is
business as usual as far as civil politics is concerned. And they continue operating under the assumption that we can get democracy
back on track. That doesn't work when only one party is striving
for that end.

We're not playing the same game. There is plenty of evidence
that the two parties have their eyes trained on entirely different
goals. Think no further than Republican efforts to wreck the
government so that they can point at it and shout that it's broken,
or the norms they have kicked to the curb.* One party is seeking
power and dominance by any means necessary. The other is
attempting to see democracy flourish.

It's not without consequence that only one of those is abetted
by their own haven for unchecked coverage. Many people still
believe that our "leftward-leaning" media provides a balanced
equivalent to the collective forces of Fox, Newsmax, OANN, the

---

* In the form of emoluments violations, appointing family members to advisory roles,
attacking voting rights, imposing restrictions on reproductive rights and even seeking
to prevent interstate travel to enforce those restrictions, appointing unqualified judges,
trying to prohibit *all* immigration, abandoning NATO allies, coddling dictators, abusing
the power of impeachment, and inciting an insurrection at the Capitol. And that's the
short list.

Daily Wire, and the vast array of emerging influencers offering a demographic of primarily young white men an on-ramp to far-right conservatism.

It's not equivalent.

Heather Cox Richardson feels that "the safe haven of false equivalence led the press to ignore one of the most consequential developments in contemporary American politics: the radicalization of the Republican Party." There's no equivalent on the left. To those who don't see this, or believe otherwise, I'll nod back to the incessant lies, slander, propaganda, and consequent lawsuits that have defined the rights' news outlets. And when it comes to whether this is an apples-to-apples media landscape, let's remember Sean Hannity's nightcap chats with Trump. I will very happily reopen the debate of equivalency as soon as Biden starts calling Rachel Maddow every evening for a strategy sesh, morale boost, and bedtime story.

OF COURSE, A HOPEFUL NUMBER OF PIONEERS HAVE LAUNCHED early efforts to create content for our progressive media ecosystem, and a promising showing of politicians have proved that they are in fact not stuck in amber, and have been willing to embrace independent sources for sharing their message. The Trump White House and the Biden White House have shown that they appreciate and understand the value of an ideologically aligned media ecosystem. That's to the credit of both, considering how rigid and change-resistant that space's relationship has been to the press historically.

Naturally, they had different motivations.

Trump rarely did interviews with outlets other than Fox. His first chief strategist, Steve Bannon, sat down with the *New York*

Times at the beginning of Trump's term and made it perfectly clear how he felt about legacy media. "The media here is the opposition party. They don't understand this country." His scathing attacks on the *Times*[*] and on any "elite" or "mainstream" media outlet would have been an opinion shared with and emphasized to Trump, who was by that stage already enraged with any source that hadn't lied about the sad turnout at his inauguration.

When Trump was president and tweeting at all hours, he was also bolstering and promoting articles from digital chums like *The Washington Free Beacon* and *The Federalist.* He scratched their back; they scratched his.[†] But by promoting their work, he was offering a strong vote of validation, not to mention exposure, among his staggeringly large base.

What he was doing, Pfeiffer noted, was "laying hands on these media entities, but he's also making them money because he's sending them traffic, which is allowing them to exist." The same exchange of favors was applied to books. "Donald Trump spent a ton of time promoting the books of conservative writers who were writing pro-Trump books. The value of that is he was trying to get them on the *New York Times* bestseller list—then those authors get to do more TV interviews, more newspaper interviews, get more coverage, but also publishers want to sign more authors who are going to write pro-Trump books." All of it served his ravenous ego while expanding his base. He helped himself while also invigorating the conservative media ecosystem. Any channel that would be less inclined to fact-check him, more inclined to show him loyalty, and less inclined to hold his bone spurs to the fire was his kind of space.

---

[*] Which Bannon admitted he has been reading for most of his adult life.

[†] Gross. Sorry.

THE DAY KETANJI BROWN JACKSON WAS NOMINATED TO THE position of associate justice of the Supreme Court, and just one day after Russia invaded Ukraine, the Biden administration welcomed me and Heather Cox Richardson to the White House. We both worked outside of legacy media, with followings cultivated entirely through social media. We had been invited to conduct separate interviews with the president. It was a radical decision, as that kind of access is so often hoarded by the mainstream media (which suggests that it's perhaps politicians' responsibility to broaden that access).

Pfeiffer noted that the benefits go both ways: "I was so excited when President Biden sat down with you. He gives you credibility, gives you attention, builds up your audience—in addition to benefiting himself."

But those advantages notwithstanding, independent media figures perhaps serve as an alternative to a mainstream media ecosystem whose support from the public has eroded. "That idea of creating spaces where people are is hugely important," said Richardson, "because if you look at the recent statistics, which suggest that Americans don't trust the government, that came from forty years of the radical right telling people not to trust the government. . . . I think the future of our media is here on the fringes, but we are rapidly becoming the center.

"It's partly that they don't trust the government. But I also think there's something else that speaks to the new media, like us . . . Putting your heart behind something is much more difficult than saying, 'I don't believe you.' . . . So I think what the White House was doing in that time was recognizing that people who were not part of the legacy media might be more willing to get on board with the principles that Biden has been trying to embrace since he took office."

If the White House (which—when it comes to the press—is historically as nimble as a cruise ship) can adapt, there is no reason the entire political space can't recognize the virtues of a robust independent media ecosystem.

The pursuit of progress demands that we support independent, progressive media. (I know, I know, the guy with a YouTube channel encourages more support of people with YouTube channels.) Mainstream media feels too conflicted about advocating for Democrats without qualifying that advocacy to the ends of the earth. That's their prerogative. But it only underscores the importance of having an ecosystem that *does* recognize the value of advocating for progressive causes and the politicians who fight for them.

A major reason why people don't know what Biden has done or how profoundly their vote matters returns us to shifts in the media ecosystem that make it increasingly hard for people to access that information with ease. We need to create a new infrastructure to disseminate essential intel and inspiration. That is precisely why I started creating video content.

I vividly remember being on Facebook in 2018.* Video was only just starting to catch on, but right away I began noticing that I was exclusively being served right-wing content on the platform. It was rife with straw man arguments and logical fallacies and straight-up, dangerous lies. And what's worse, there was effectively no one on the left rebutting it. My options were either to wait for our white knights in the mainstream media to figure out the emergent medium of video and start pushing back on the certifiable deluge of disinformation (fast), or to do it myself.

---

* Before my parents' generation fully pried it from our millennial grasp, inundating it with photos of dogs, cats, and grandchildren as profile pictures.

I had zero background in video production, but I was in Los Angeles to be an actor (ostensibly—even if those damn casting directors weren't having it), so I knew I could manage well enough in front of a camera. My first videos were blurry and blown-out and badly cropped and poorly sound-designed, and my suit was too big and my hair was even bigger and my pacing was at a crawl.* But I eventually fixed the technical stuff and bought clothes that fit and got a haircut; meanwhile, the videos caught fire.

Within two years, my YouTube channel hit one million subscribers, and within another two years, the channel hit one billion views. While I'd love to believe that I single-handedly revolutionized the digital political media space, the truth is that there was (and remains) a dearth in progressive voices—an appetite for anything that wasn't either right-wing propaganda or content twisting itself into pretzels to pander to those very propagandists. There was clear exhaustion with and waning trust in legacy media; my channel's success is due in part to that.

But it isn't enough. We need more voices. We need to get organized.

The right's infrastructure is deeper and wider; it spans the more traditional digital outlets, like YouTube and Facebook and podcasts, and the new ones, like TikTok and Discord servers. Hasan addressed the fact that liberals don't have a tightly coordinated or intentional presence across those platforms, despite the clear demographic advantages they offer.

"Obviously, TikTok is a more liberal place than a conservative place, but that's more of a generational issue, not because the left or liberals have invested money in strategizing on how to take over

---

* Don't bother trying to find them; I have made sure that they won't see the light of day.

Instagram and TikTok." His conviction about the importance of independent media is tied to the great role it could play in terms of "helping shape the Democratic Party in the way that the right wing has done with the Republican Party; providing Democrats with some kind of 'echo chamber' in the way that Republicans have; and in providing young people—who are crucial to Democratic Party prospects and are pretty pissed off right now—with an opportunity to engage with some kind of coordinated messaging that's not ad hoc."

These elections will be waged and won not in mainstream outlets but on emerging platforms. It won't be Walter Cronkite who informs our decisions; it will be trusted voices on TikTok and Instagram, communities on message boards and servers, friends chatting on iMessage and WhatsApp and Snapchat.

It's likely too late for Democrats to recover their losses as far as legacy media is concerned, but the independent space is only just beginning to gain its footing. We've witnessed how the right's dedicated media ecosystem has paid dividends in buttressing a political party that has decidedly poor messaging, poor ideas, and poor spokespeople. Knowing the staggering benefits conferred to one side wins when they have a monopoly on distribution, we cannot afford to surrender the next generation of media.

We especially cannot afford to surrender it now, at such a pivotal moment. As President Biden underscored in our interview, "I said at the outset of my presidency that we're at a genuine inflection point in world history. It occurs every three or four or five generations, the fundamental change taking place in the world." Our present inflection point is a tug-of-war, and on one side is a Republican Party largely intent on embracing authoritarianism, waging disinformation campaigns, and exploiting electoral processes without regard for consequence. On the other side are those who haven't given up on democracy and no longer want to exist in a constant state of *what happens if we become a dictatorship*.

Could any of us have predicted what a dangerous time we'd be living through in the U.S., or how essential it would become that we all do our part? Amid global shifts toward authoritarian regimes, many uninitiated Americans, especially those not terribly involved in politics, are not getting the message. Instead, they're getting snippets of the president's gaffes and relentless references to his age, shared along with the implicit suggestion that these are—in any world—analogous to his opponent's propensity for committing egregious crimes and abusing power.

Nonsense aside (a tall order, I know), it's empowering to live through a period of such consequence, when so many disparate voices are shared publicly. But with that comes a fiercer reliance on being cautious and vigilant about the tsunami of utter bullshit that is now available to the American public. It will pay dividends to have some grasp on the peril of what a faction of anti-democratic arsonists have done, can do, and will do when they find themselves together frothing for power.

7

THE DISLOYAL OPPOSITION

On the evening of January 20, 2009, revelers from all over the world gathered in Washington, DC, to celebrate Barack Obama's victory. It was the night of the inaugural balls, and the closed-off streets were packed. The mood was ebullient. People engaged with strangers, telling stories about the journeys they had taken to be there to witness history, crying tears of joy, surveying fellow celebrants' faces, sharing in the excitement that comes with the fulfillment of an audacious hope.

At the same time, top members of the Republican Party were gathering downtown at a swanky steakhouse called the Caucus Room. Each time the door opened, the sounds of a rejoicing city clashed with the arrival of yet another despondent Republican politician. Eventually, over a dozen figures took their seats around the table. Included among the gathering were top conservative lawmakers Eric Cantor, Kevin McCarthy, and Paul Ryan, as well as several ranking members of the Senate. The lights were dim, the voices were muted enough to hear ice cracking in tumblers; an air of hopelessness loomed large.

But by the end of the night, the mood had shifted. Full of dry-aged steaks and bourbon and settled on a shared plan of attack against the new president, the pack of recently somber lawmakers would emerge as jubilant as the street revelers who surrounded them. But the hope they felt was of a different, far more cynical variety. What transpired in that room would have implications that would last well beyond the nascent presidency of Barack Obama.

The event had been organized by Frank Luntz. "I cannot begin to tell you what an amazing euphoric moment that was for so many people," Luntz said, in the *Frontline* documentary *Divided States of America.** "It really was a coming-together. It really was America at its best." Of course, that stood in stark contrast to the mood on the right: "I think that the Republican situation was as bad as on the day Richard Nixon resigned. Everyone was depressed."

Obama had campaigned on a message of hope, change, and unity: sentiments and promises that served as powerful antidotes to the obstruction and rancor that Republicans had offered. With his election, people across the country felt a sense of promise in politics.

Republicans were terrified by such optimism. The boys in the Caucus Room were frightened by not just the potency of it but also what it had yielded: roughly nine million more Americans had voted in that election and entered the democratic process. Minorities and young people had turned out in droves. The new coalition inspired by Obama threatened the GOP on an existential level.

Most of the Republicans in attendance that night had experienced firsthand the wonder of Obama's inauguration. As they looked out at the over 1.5 million exuberant attendees on the

---

* From which all of the quotes about that evening were taken.

Mall, according to journalist and author Robert Draper, it "felt like a wholesale repudiation of the Republican Party. It felt like a force with which they couldn't reckon, and perhaps not even comprehend."

After all, they hadn't just lost the presidency. They lost all the Senate seats they were vying for, along with multiple seats in the House, and—with those losses—any definitive claim over, or certainty about, what the future would look like in Washington, DC. The combination of turnout and enthusiasm was so overwhelming that, even for a party that strives for minority rule, they were devastated. With a tidal change and progressive current as strong as any of them had ever felt, they marinated in the grim likelihood that it would take generations for their party to recover (or, more importantly, for them to feel powerful again).

One of the most conniving minds of the Republican Party was on hand to offer instruction. Newt Gingrich led off the discussion, because—as Luntz later claimed—it made sense to hear from the former Speaker of the House, someone "who could encapsulate the challenges of what it was to be a very small minority and an insignificant one, and how you, through whatever kind of strategy or planning, create the ingredients to at some point become the majority."

"The point I made," Gingrich said, swelling with delight as he remembered mentoring all those small and insignificant men, "was that we had to be prepared, in the tradition of [Coach John] Wooden at UCLA, to run a full court press. . . . If Obama governed from the center, we'd have one set of realities. If he governed from the left, we'd have a different set. . . . we had to see what evolved. . . . we had to be responsive. You know, our job was to be the loyal opposition and to . . . offer an alternative to what he wanted to do."

The problem with Gingrich's claim is that being the "loyal opposition" (an eighteenth-century British term) is supposed to mean "that a party in opposition is loyal to the same fundamental interests and principles as the party in power." That part must have escaped them, because when the Republicans left that evening, they had settled on a strategy of total opposition. Despite the global economic crisis the government urgently needed to address, these men resolved to reject everything their new president might propose. None of his legislative initiatives would get their support. None.

Gingrich reasoned that Obama "could be defeated partly by his own ideology and by his own behaviors," before coming to an even more insidious realization. "By the end of the evening, you began to reorient and realize, 'Wait a second, you got Nancy Pelosi as an opponent. You have a clear choice of ideologies. We have a tremendous amount of hard work to do, but it's doable."

What Gingrich and the others had decided was doable was *not* working across the aisle to better American lives. It was *not* adding jobs, nor was it fixing a broken economy—despite the reality that the country was basically in the throes of one of its worst economic downturns in history. It was *not* expanding health care, even though Obama was clear about his intention to do just that. The "tremendous amount of hard work" was solely intended to employ whatever finite resources were at their disposal to oppose Obama and the Democrats.

The strategy was clear:

Oppose. Establish dysfunction. Blame the others.

This wasn't just a pinkie-swear decision drummed up by a few deflated cronies at the end of a long day. Mitch McConnell, chief thwarter of the Obama agenda, had already had his own meeting and come up with the same strategy of how to sabotage the country's welfare for partisan gain.

Within a week of the inauguration, Obama's immediate attention was focused on accomplishing two exceedingly ambitious goals in the wake of a calamitous Bush presidency, marred by war and financial collapse: rescue a shattered economy, and do so by joining hands with Republicans.

Obama offered bipartisan solutions within a matter of days, going so far as to speak exclusively to the Republicans in an effort to sell his stimulus bill. But they had already established their strategy: opposition. Speaker Nancy Pelosi recalls how evident it was that, prior to the meeting, McConnell, Cantor, and other members of the Republican leadership had informed their party, "We're not for any of it, no matter what it is. No. Just say no." As former Republican Senator George Voinovich explained, "If he was for it . . . we had to be against it." Obama had promised the country bipartisanship. If there was any of that on display, America would credit the president. The GOP couldn't possibly have that.

Not one single Republican voted for the stimulus bill, despite accommodations that Obama had made *for them*. It would pass anyway in the Democrat-led House, but the message had been sent by the GOP. His gestures didn't matter. He'd earned himself no goodwill. There would be no compromise. Though Obama and his administration accomplished an *extraordinary* amount under those circumstances, his agenda was left unfinished.

The Republicans followed through on the most cowardly decision of all: that theirs would be the Party of No. Unfortunately, that legacy has held strong.

FIFTEEN YEARS LATER, THE PHILOSOPHY OF ANTAGONISM IS hardwired into the Party of No. They have eschewed all other priorities in their nonstop efforts to fuck things up while pursuing power: Republicans openly court white supremacists and neo-Nazis, who now march proudly down our streets. They constantly bring the government to the brink of shutdown. They encourage Russia to meddle in our elections and launder their disinformation for their own political gain. They turn public health crises into culture wars. They pass draconian legislation while activist judges uphold their theocratic agenda. They wield the threat of violence as a political tool. They casually employ racist tropes and deny the existence of slavery.

And their treasonous behavior is not only commonplace, it's lionized.

It took fifteen years, but Gingrich and company are now realizing the full potential of the Pandora's box they opened. All the while, the country has been split into two distinct teams for whom conflict, friction, opposition, hostility, and acrimony are not only expected but permanent.

When our politics seems irrevocably broken, one political party does actually derive a benefit. The Republicans want a government so small that it's "reduce[d] . . . to the size where I can drag it into the bathroom and drown it in the bathtub," as Grover Norquist infamously quipped. The way Republicans seek to sell that idea to the American public is by *breaking* the government, thereby proving that it cannot function, *and so we might as well starve the beast in hopes that eventually it dies.* And when it does die, it'll be those "small government conservatives" waiting in the wings to swoop into power with an "I told you so" attitude.

When those Republicans met in the Caucus Room in January 2009, they understood that helping Barack Obama and the Democrats would ultimately hurt their cause—namely, securing their own power and relevance. They opted for a different route and together sought to facilitate dysfunction, sow distrust, and help themselves.

Preserving that acrimony has become a deeply held principle in today's GOP. Donald Trump's ascendancy in the party is a testament to exactly that. He is a human wrecking ball, the symbol of a diseased party reliant on destruction as a political strategy.

And as we have seen, there is a fully formed, ready-made eco-system in place to prop up Republicans, sell their lies as truth, and vilify their opponents across coordinated print, television, and social media programming. Ever since the Republicans' "decidedly more confrontational and dogmatic"* media rumbled into dom-inance, Democrats' appearances have been weaponized, mocked ruthlessly, and spun out of context. It's an ecosystem designed to preclude communication between the two sides, precisely because exacerbating those tensions is the point.

It's not until a Democrat enters their arena that the Republicans' elaborate fiction suddenly becomes threatened. A few brave souls on the left have been willing to enter the fray. In late 2023, Governor Gavin Newsom engaged in a debate on Fox News (moderated by the not-quite-impartial Sean Hannity) with Governor Ron DeSantis. While DeSantis's usual media appearances are carefully curated to make him seem tough (during the pandemic, he opted to berate students at a public press conference for the *crime* of wearing masks to protect themselves), his debate with Newsom culminated in the Florida governor desperately showcasing a "poop map."† It was not a gesture that implied victory.

---

* Framed as such in a *Washington Post* opinion piece about how "Conservatives Owe Limbaugh a Debt of Gratitude."

† What DeSantis described as "an app where they plot the human feces that are found on the streets of San Francisco."

Jessica Tarlov is Fox's token liberal who more than holds her own against her conservative co-hosts on *The Five*, on which she is outnumbered four to one. My favorite moment took place during a discussion of the COVID vaccine, when Tarlov was interrupted by Judge Jeanine (Jeanine Pirro):

TARLOV: *You need to find some safe middle ground where people know that the vaccine is safe for you—*

JUDGE JEANINE: *Ugh.*

TARLOV: *Ugh? What do you mean? You're fine. You're vaccinated. Why are you "ugh-ing"?*

Judge Jeanine, like a deer in headlights, doesn't say a word.

TARLOV: *It's your turn.*

Embarrassed, smirking, Tarlov's opponent squeaks out her response.

JUDGE JEANINE: *It's your—it's your segment.*

It sure is inconvenient when Fox's audience (groomed into believing that the vaccine is the root of all evil) gets let in on the secret: all of those hosts will avail themselves of the very protection they're working hard to deny their viewers.

NO ONE, HOWEVER, DOES IT MORE EFFECTIVELY THAN PETE Buttigieg.

In October 2022, Buttigieg appeared on Fox and was asked to humor that day's dose of idiocy served up by Marjorie Taylor Greene:

NEIL CAVUTO: *Marjorie Taylor Greene, the Georgia Republican, at a rally in Michigan said this past weekend that Mr. Buttigieg is trying to emasculate the way we drive by supporting environmentally friendly transportation. But what did you think of her wording?*

BUTTIGIEG: *I literally don't even understand what that means. I mean, my sense of manhood is not connected to whether my vehicle is fueled by gasoline or whether it's fueled by electricity—*

CAVUTO: *Were you offended by that, sir? Because even people who share her politics didn't share that view.*

BUTTIGIEG: *It was a strange thing to say. You know, to be honest, there are other members of Congress that I pay more attention to when I'm thinking about opinions that really matter or ideas that are going to be critical to engage with. I do think we need to zoom out a little bit. I know people want to make this ideological, they want to make it political. We're talking about something like electric vehicles. We're talking, again, about a very practical matter, which is how we get from point A to point B. And if industry and the world are moving in the direction that adopts a new technology, the real question is: are we going to let China lead that or are we going to lead it here in the United States of America?*

Greene's homophobic implication was clear, but if anyone was emasculated here—if anyone's talking points were castrated—it was Greene.

Just as impressive as his level-toned dismissal of Greene is the deftness with which Buttigieg pivots back on message. While many people (myself included) enjoy the filleting, I'm sure many *more* people care that their tax dollars are being managed competently. Buttigieg is able to satiate both styles of viewers.

In January 2023 he appeared alongside Fox's Bret Baier. This time, Baier himself decided to take on the mantle of ignorant interlocutor.

> BAIER: *You also brought your husband, Chasten, on a military aircraft to attend a sporting event in the Netherlands. Was that reimbursed? Because that was one of the controversies with the price.*

> BUTTIGIEG: *Of course not. I led a presidential delegation to support American wounded warriors and injured service members—the Invictus Games—as has been tradition for many years. I led the American delegation as one of the great honors of my time in this job. And the diplomatic protocol on a presidential delegation is that the principal is often accompanied by their spouse. It was a great trip. It was incredible. It was also a few weeks into the Ukraine war, so we had a chance at the U.S. embassy to engage with the Ukrainian competitors, also wounded service members. Some of them went from the games back to the battlefield to fight for their country. I also took the opportunity to sit with the Prime Minister of the Netherlands to look at Dutch port infrastructure. But here's what I want you to understand. Before me, it was the Secretary of the Army under President Trump who took that trip with his wife. Before that it was Mrs. Trump as First Lady who went to the Invictus Games. Before that, Mrs. Obama did the same thing—*

BAIER: *Sure—*

BUTTIGIEG: *And I guess the question on my mind is if no one's raising questions about why Secretary Esper and his wife led that delegation—*

BAIER: *No—*

BUTTIGIEG:—*as well they should have, then why is it any different when it's me and my husband?*

BAIER: *Understood.*

All of us have experienced at least one moment in our lives where it would be convenient for the earth to simply open up and swallow us whole. Unfortunately for Bret Baier, few of us have that moment broadcast on national television.

Buttigieg's skill is not just the fact that he's able to deftly dodge and dismantle the usual pelting of right-wing disinformation and expose its inane logic. The danger of someone like Buttigieg, as far as Republicans are concerned, is that he has been able to transcend what conservative and (much of) mainstream media is trying to impress upon the country: a reinforced notion that we are an irreparably polarized nation.

"The great irony is that on almost every major policy issue, a strong majority of Americans agree with Democrats and disagree with the Republicans," Buttigieg said. "Most people tend to agree on things like marriage, certainly choice, as well as discrimination," he explained to me.

Indeed, despite what we may hear from our local diner booth–inhabiting, MAGA hat–wearing "patriots" omnipresent in media coverage, *most Americans tend to agree.*

A majority of Americans continually reveal at the ballot boxes that they are pro-choice. A majority support commonsense gun safety measures. A majority want to see the ultrawealthy pay their fair share. A majority support a living wage. A majority support labor unions. A majority support confronting climate change, if not for our generation, then for their children and grandchildren's generations. And a majority support a society that is multicultural, so that as a country we can thrive amid diverse perspectives and live up to the idea of America.

Even with all their opposers, all their nay votes, all their dysfunction, Republicans are lacking in the most powerful weapon of all: consensus. It's a weapon that the GOP has spent decades trying to destroy by fanning the flames of partisanship—which is to say nothing of the catastrophic contribution Trump has made to keep those flames raging.

Messages of unity are rarely covered by any media outlet. The absolute last place you'll receive such shocking news is from the right, whose enthusiasm would plummet if everything were running smoothly. A political party whose identity is predicated on shrinking government and saying *no* to any and all progressive policy needs to sell the impression that our system is steeped in permanent dysfunction and our populace locked in a perpetual stalemate.

Which is why there's particular danger for Republicans in someone like Buttigieg, who sees each interviewer not as a right-wing media apparatchik but rather "as a friend or relative that I might be sparring in a friendly way with over things that we both care about. Because that's part of the mindset, if not of the host then certainly their viewer."

Buttigieg reasons that if he's able to reach somebody who relies on conservative media outlets as their top or *only* source of information, he's willing to take a chance to get a message to them. "Does it legitimize media with questionable practices? There is that risk, but for a very large portion of the public, their legitimacy is not in question. So you're not changing hearts and minds by staying out of it," he said.

Democrats may not have an equivalent distribution system in place, but we do have the power to offer much more positive news. We've even proven that we can get behind "hope and change," especially when the alternative is dictatorship "on day one."

Buttigieg doesn't tend to bang people over the head with talking points; nor does he get bogged down in questions of platforms or messaging. If you want to know what Democrats' brand is, look around and absorb the reality. "Instead of saying, 'Here's who we are as Democrats, look at us,'" said Buttigieg, "it's, 'Look around *you*. Look at how much you're paying for insulin. Look at your rights—especially for women right now. We're with you on this.'" And the more people start paying attention to such improvement, the closer we will get to reclaiming the greatest weapon there is for battling Republicans: a hopeful democratic body.

Granted, I've worked in the media long enough to know that it's a hell of a lot more challenging to attract eyeballs to a discussion of antitrust legislation than to, say, a Republican congresswoman's heavy petting session inside a crowded theater during a performance of *Beetlejuice* before she is frog-marched out and shouts, "Do you know who I am?"

I get it. The comparatively boring work of policy, progress, and governing struggles to compete with the sensationalist entertainment of Republican histrionics. "There have been moments when the Democratic Party lost its way," Buttigieg concedes, "but the Republican Party has lost its mind. And we can't go on like that." Which is why he contends that there's a "readiness—maybe even a hunger—for a lot of people to open their computer or turn on the TV and have something other than poison on display."

It's crucial for voices like Pete Buttigieg to be willing to transcend the partisan media divide; after all, voters can only be persuaded if they hear from us. And beyond that, it helps viewers to understand that the enemy here isn't each other (again, Americans largely agree); it's the people who've created a system designed to foster hostility for their own partisan gain.

The natural conclusion of the 1971 Powell memo, the aggressive blueprint that forever changed the influence of big business on our cultural and political landscape, was the consolidation of power for Republicans. It established the relationship between the parties as a battle, and instructed that survival was predicated on being the first to attack. More than half a century later, opposition, dysfunction, and that attack mentality are the only true ideals of the Republican party and its press. The "poison on display" that Buttigieg alluded to is what keeps that system in place.

The point of a progressive media is not to create our version of Fox for the left. We're not looking for a left-wing equivalent to the Powell memo. We're not trying to match their model of perpetual hostility. Those things were designed to serve a failing party that exists to destroy the government. We're fighting to preserve it.

And while I accept that in many ways we are a broken body, that body has been broken by the strategy of *very few people*. Democrats have the leaders, the consensus, and the numbers to overcome such cynicism. They don't have to go by the Republican playbook. They don't have to wage attacks and facilitate despondency and leave people thinking that nothing in government works. That's not Democrats' brand. Democrats don't have to follow the Republican path or use their tools of manipulation and division. That only leads off the cliff, and only serves to help keep in place the pernicious scheme conjured up in the Caucus Room all those years ago.

We have all the tools necessary to reclaim our democracy from those who are seeking to destroy it. But we'll never be able to achieve that until we recognize our own agency in this battle.

8

POKING HOLES IN POTATOES

"I fight because I am trying to buy time for democracy," Marc Elias said. "I'm not trying to fix it. People who think I am fixing it are giving me and my litigation way too much credit. We are buying time because as soon as we strike down a law in court, they can go ahead and pass a new one. So I'm trying to buy time for democracy without an end goal of how that time will fix things— barring, say, a voting rights act.

"The other reason that I fight is much more personal. I come from a background of people who have always faced the possibility of the end of liberalism or democracy, depending on the era. It's hard to say that tsarist Russia was liberal or democratic, or that prewar Germany was. So let's say I come from a background of people who have always had to worry about whether or not the fate of government would turn against them, or whether the space that they had achieved in civil society would contract."

Elias studied for his bar mitzvah in 1982, engaging with middle-aged Holocaust survivors who had been in the camps when they were in their twenties, and with American war veterans. Of his mentors, the person "with the greatest impact on me," said Elias, "was not a Holocaust survivor. He was actually a guy who was a

Jewish American who had fought in World War II for the United States. This was just a regular guy who was eighteen or nineteen years old and was drafted. . . . But then he found himself captured by the Nazis. So he was terrified, of course, because he was sent to a German stalag (POW camp). . . . He talked to us about what that experience was like. Despite the laws of war, the Germans identified the Jewish prisoners and gave them work detail. This guy was put onto doing agricultural work.

"He and a bunch of the other Jewish prisoners got this idea to take little pieces of barbed wire, which they could find around the camp. They decided they would use those little pieces of wire to poke holes in the produce before they delivered it, with the idea that it would spoil the potatoes. So they all went out there, picked and processed the potatoes, then would take barbed wire and surreptitiously poke holes, in the hopes that the potatoes would rot. Their rationale was that in doing so, they would starve the Nazi army. The produce would get sent to the army, and then the German soldiers would have nothing but rotten potatoes to eat, and they would starve.

"That image has always stayed in my head. Some nineteen-year-old American who had ended up in a Nazi stalag, segregated with other Jews, and they all took razor wire with their bare hands . . . and there he was, just repetitively poking holes in potatoes all day with bloody fingers, thinking that the net effect of that was going to be that the Nazis would starve in the war effort.

"I feel like I owe that to our democracy. I'm going to poke holes in the potatoes. Maybe it won't matter at all. Maybe none of these cases I'm taking, in the end, will be the thing that keeps Donald Trump from getting back in office. Maybe it'll be a landslide election one way or the other, but—while I'm here, while I can—I'm just going to keep poking holes until there are no more potatoes to poke."

IT'S DIFFICULT NOT TO FEEL HELPLESS AS FAR AS POLITICS IS concerned. How could we not? Just look at the forces we're contending with: a right-wing disinformation machine, a Republican Party that is fundamentally opposed to democracy, conservative lawyers content to abuse the judicial system, and far-right legislators unwilling or unable to feel shame. The fact that Mitch McConnell—*Mitch McConnell*—is right now considered not sufficiently conservative is a testament to just how far and how fast the Overton window is shifting. McConnell, whose swan song we are witnessing in 2024, is unquestionably the individual most responsible for the hard right Supreme Court majority that revoked the constitutional right to abortion, gutted affirmative action, and generally tried to return the country to the nineteenth century. That his politics and methods seem moderate relative to his colleagues' politics and methods underscores the extremism at work and the danger that poses for the country.

So if you're feeling a sense of helplessness in the system, *take comfort* in knowing that all of this was designed to foster and cultivate that instinct. But also . . . *get horrified* with the knowledge that it was designed to foster and cultivate that instinct.

As we have seen, the strategy is as deliberate as it is insidious. Losing faith and abandoning the system altogether redounds to Republicans' electoral benefit. That's how they want you to respond. The way to counter their cynical tactics is to recognize that your participation is not only necessary but majorly impactful. The antidote to helplessness is the recognition of your own agency—

and a willingness to use it. Nothing could hurt the Republicans more profoundly than a public demonstrating a restored faith in our numbers, our leaders, and our government.

In both the 2016 and 2020 election cycles, Wisconsin is believed by many to have been the tipping point state whose votes were responsible for resolving the election. In both of those elections, Wisconsin's winner—Trump in 2016 and Biden in 2020—was decided by about *two votes per precinct*. Not thousands, not hundreds, not even tens; per precinct, you and the first person you see when you look up from this page would have been enough to change the outcomes of the presidential election if you voted in Wisconsin.

In fact, margins that small have swung elections for decades. In 2000, George W. Bush defeated Al Gore by 537 votes in Florida, tipping the state in that election (and saddling us with an agenda that prioritized the Iraq War over climate action).

In 2020, Republican Mariannette Miller-Meeks defeated Democrat Rita Hart by only 6 votes in Iowa's Second Congressional District, helping further narrow the Democrats' razor-thin 222–213 House majority.

In 2022, Democrat Kris Mayes defeated Abraham Hamadeh, a Republican election denier, by 280 votes to become attorney general of Arizona. The state is in many ways the epicenter of Republican attacks against elections. As such, it benefits greatly from having someone who accepts the core tenets of democracy in the AG's office.

In 2018, Republican David Yancey tied with Democrat Shelly Simonds, 11,607–11,607, in the race for House District Ninety-Four in the Virginia House of Delegates. Per Virginia law, the winner would be selected by a random drawing. On January 4, 2018, an official of the Virginia State Board of

Elections pulled Yancey's name from a ceramic bowl—and with it handed Republicans control of the state House of Delegates by a margin of 51 to 49. A single vote could have changed control of one entire chamber of the Virginia state legislature.

Further underscoring the importance of every vote: Because we're living in an era of hyper-polarization, the number of competitive races has been dropping every cycle. In 2018, forty-four House races were decided within a 5 percent margin. That number dropped to thirty-nine races in 2020 and thirty-six races in 2022. Meanwhile, the number of victories by a margin of 20 percent or more jumped from 265 in 2018 to 291 in 2022. According to Pew Research, "After a long run of comfortably large Democratic House majorities from the late 1950s through the early 1990s, narrow majorities—defined for this analysis as margins of control of fewer than 5 percentage points—have prevailed in a third of the 15 most recent Houses." Vice President Kamala Harris has already made history by casting the greatest number of tie-breaking votes in U.S. history, surpassing John C. Calhoun, John Adams, George M. Dallas, Schuyler Colfax, George Clinton, and Richard Mentor Johnson—none of whom served after the nineteenth century.

Outcomes like these, with presidential elections and other consequential elections won by just a couple of votes per precinct or a few hundred votes statewide or even by drawing a name out of a bowl, point to the fact that our participation matters. And as the number of truly competitive races falls, our participation has never mattered more.

Granted, there are plenty of people who are skeptical of this.

My mom was never interested in politics. For my entire life, she never voted. Even when I was a doe-eyed teenager demanding that she explain to me her indifference about climate change or raising wages or fixing immigration, I always got the same answer. It went something like, "They're all corrupt! They're all on the same team! They don't care about us, they care about themselves. I don't have time for any of this shit. I have to wake up at five o'clock in the morning to go to work."

And indeed, at five o'clock in the morning, she would drive to the labor and delivery unit of the hospital for her thirteen-hour shift.

My attempts to proselytize grew fewer and further between, as every time I suggested that perhaps we might have some agency in our country's future, I was met with the same script: "They're all crooks. They don't give a shit about us. I gotta go to work in the morning."

When I started my YouTube channel, my mom would watch my videos—solely, I thought, so that she could complain that I was cutting my hair too short. I eventually grew busy warning my viewers about the clear and present danger of the modern GOP—so busy that I no longer had time to continue trying to persuade my obstinate mother of the same thing.

A few days before the 2020 election, I got a text from my mom, which I assumed would be some iteration of a reminder that I consume food and perhaps even sleep. I opened the text to a photo of her standing at a ballot drop box outside of the local post office in my Jersey hometown, ballot in hand. After refusing to vote for over sixty years, she had cast her vote for Joe Biden and Democrats straight down the ballot.

I know—I convinced my own mother to vote; *what an accomplishment*. But the thing about a Jewish mother from Brooklyn is that I would have more luck convincing the sun to rise at night than urging her to do anything against her will. You think you know what stubborn is; I assure you, you do not.

Of course, seeing the numbers of people watching my videos is rewarding, but it pales in comparison to moments like that one. Knowing that I had influenced the actual vote of one person who otherwise wouldn't have bothered casting her ballot—made that much sweeter because it was the world's most emphatic skeptic— meant so much more to me than the usual rewards of social media, like a viral video.

You don't need a big social media following to make an impact; you don't need *any* social media following. It's not about reaching *everyone*; it's about reaching *someone*. If I could get a woman obstinate enough to categorically shun a restaurant for life because she didn't like their food that one time in 1997 to renounce her lifelong abstention from voting, then anyone can be persuaded. We all have that family member, that friend, that coworker, that neighbor who just doesn't care or who thinks that voting doesn't matter. Be responsible for that person. The margins on which these elections are won or lost are composed of them.

For me, the point of having a following on social media is not to create some closed-loop ecosystem. My videos aren't the end of the pipeline; they're the beginning. Only a small fraction of my job is persuading the people who actively choose to watch my videos. Those viewers ended up there for a reason; they sought out the content or clicked on the link ostensibly because their opinion already aligns with mine. The real significance of my work is to arm viewers with the tools necessary to persuade *their* circles. That's where the real difference is made: when my viewers take the message to people in their lives who wouldn't have sought out my work otherwise— perhaps because they don't use YouTube or they disagree with my perspective or they think politics is a hopeless endeavor.

Word of mouth has always been essential to the electoral process, and in an era when the share of voters who are truly up for grabs is shrinking every year, those personal connections are becoming that much more valuable. It's how we reach the folks who don't vote or who haven't formed their opinions yet. As Dan Pfeiffer states, "We're only going to reach voters through a whole bunch of people who act as sort of tribunes for our message."

That strategy is so potent that it was the entire basis for Jen Psaki's famous sparring matches with Fox's Peter Doocy. "Was I going to win over all of the Fox audience? No," she laughed. "Many of them think I'm the devil incarnate. But it was more about equipping people who might be having similar arguments with what they could say. So thinking about how to explain things in a clear, fact-based way, where people can say, 'I heard that, Uncle Joe, and actually that's not true because of X, Y, and Z.' That's how I always thought about it.

"I also think, and this is tricky, but when I was at the White House, it was during a stage when we were following Trump, and having a daily 'we're going to ignore Fox' battle. I didn't think that was going to be constructive. Neither did the president. We don't need that to be what people are focused on. I did Fox News Sunday more than any other Sunday show because you don't want that to be the storyline. And frankly, a lot of what they'd ask about was predictable, because they have a rotation of stuff. So it's just about being equipped and trying to equip people who are watching with the best pushback."

It wasn't about the entertainment value (although it was entertaining), and it wasn't about schooling Peter Doocy (although he was schooled); it was about empowering tribunes to know how to deal with their own Peter Doocys. It was about arming people with the right answers so that when everyone's conservative uncle shows up at Thanksgiving dinner, one can speak with some confidence and clarity. And maybe even change some minds.

I believe my job to be important, just as Jen views her jobs (past and present) as important; both of us know that they're not nearly as important as that of the tribunes.

After Obama's victories as well as Biden's, there was a sense of mass relief, followed by a period of complacency, as though we had reached some stage of *we've won, we can take our stuff and go home*. That's a dangerous perspective—one that provides yet another kind of vacuum that Republicans can seize and distort. And they did. After Obama's triumphs, particularly in 2010, the galvanized Party of No got to work, and the left was bled dry in terms of House, Senate, and State legislative seats. Conservatives set fire to the norms governing the judiciary, and weaponized redistricting, both of which contributed to the disillusionment that ushered in Donald Trump. His term, culminating in an attempted coup at the U.S. Capitol, brought democracy to the precipice, just after much of the country had breathed a massive sigh of relief. That reality was difficult to face not just for the obvious reason but also because there was an overwhelming sense that *we'd already done so much work . . . only to end up here*. It brought on the despair that those who incited the insurrection were hoping for.

There will always be those seeking to suppress the votes of young people and people of color, to restrict ballot access, to take away drop boxes, to limit early voting and mail-in voting, to facilitate longer lines in minority-majority communities. There will always be those campaigning to strip women of their reproductive rights, or refusing to acknowledge the existence of LGBTQ+ Americans. There will always be those leading efforts to ban books but promote AR-15s. There will always be those waging disinformation campaigns and exploiting a mainstream media apparatus too easily duped by bad actors. There will always be those seeking to break the very government that the country depends upon to function. Those people will always be there.

We are never going to outright win the fight for democracy; there should always be a fight. That's what democracy is. There's power in coming to terms with that. That we'll never be able to unfurl our Mission Accomplished banner is not a capitulation to those seeking to tear democracy down; it's proof that democracy still exists. Because democracy is in the fight for democracy, always evolving and never guaranteed. Which is why Benjamin Franklin, when asked whether we had a republic or a monarchy, responded, "a republic . . . if you can keep it."

There is an entire system put in place to make you feel hopeless, exhausted, disillusioned. It's the result of years of planning and executing. It is on our television sets and our cell phones, in the courts and the polling place, the Caucus Room and the halls of Congress. And it's promulgated by a Republican Party that operates uninhibited by any sense of shame. It might feel impossible to overcome these seemingly insurmountable obstacles. But it's not; you just have to show up with the understanding that the fight will continue, and a willingness to do your part: support independent progressive media, spread the message as a tribune, be responsible for your circle, and don't let despair overwhelm hope.

You don't have to do it all. You just have to poke holes in the potatoes.

ACKNOWLEDGMENTS

While I've spent most of my career in political media quietly toiling away in solitude, this book is the product of collaboration from a wide array of amazing, supportive, and talented people, to whom I am and will remain eternally grateful.

Shameless would not exist if not for Domenica Alioto, whose genius is felt throughout the entirety of this book. I so appreciate her knowledge, expertise, and wit (not to mention knowing which darlings to kill from our 2 a.m. punch-drunk writing sessions, despite how brilliant they may have sounded to me at the time). For answering my steady stream of questions, for her endless supply of patience, for keeping the same absurd hours that I do, and for making this process so enjoyable, I am beyond thankful. I must also thank Michael Howard, who rounded out our trio of night crawlers. It was this book's incredible fortune that he helped research, fact-check, and brainstorm, and his impact cannot be overstated.

I have a mountain of gratitude for Sean Desmond, my steadfast editor, for putting so much faith in me. He transformed an otherwise intimidating prospect into an approachable and fulfilling reality. His encouragement and kindness have left a lasting impression. I must also thank the rest of the team at HarperCollins—from publisher to editor to copyeditor to production to marketing to publicity to design, and everyone in between—for their invaluable help.

I owe all the thanks in the world to my all-star agents at UTA: Marc Paskin, Pilar Queen, and Dan Milaschewski. They believed in me as an author far earlier than I ever did. There is not a moment that goes by when I don't have complete confidence that I'm in the best of hands. I simply could not ask for a better team.

This book wouldn't be half of what it is without its contributors: Pete Buttigieg, Marc Elias, Al Franken, Mehdi Hasan, Dan Pfeiffer, Jen Psaki, and Heather Cox Richardson. To have been able to collaborate on this project with people whom I admire so much has been the honor of a lifetime. They are among the very best in the business, and our democracy is stronger because of their participation in it.

I owe a special debt of gratitude to Jamie Raskin, for not only rounding out my team of contributors *and* for writing a characteristically generous and kind foreword, but for supporting me and independent media in the most deliberate way: by co-hosting our series, *Class with Jamie Raskin*. I speak for a grateful nation in expressing our undying appreciation for his contributions to this country. He is a hero of democracy.

The progressive independent media ecosystem is made that much stronger by the brilliant, talented, and dedicated coalition whom I have the privilege of working alongside. That includes Glenn Kirschner and the Team Justice community; Marc Elias, along with Blake McCarren, Sophie Feldman, and the rest of the voting rights' champions at Elias Law Group and Democracy Docket; Tim Miller and the pro-democracy voices at The Bulwark; *Pod Save America* hosts: Jon Favreau, Jon Lovett, Dan Pfeiffer, and Tommy Vietor, along with Lucinda Treat, Madeleine Haeringer, Ben Hethcoat, Elijah Cone, and all the change-makers at Crooked Media; and the inspiring team at More Perfect Union. They all deserve more credit than I could articulate for their tireless work to protect and progress our democracy.

I am especially thankful to Rashida Jones, Rebecca Kutler, Jessica Kurdali, Brad Gold, and MSNBC for taking a chance on me, introducing me to a new audience, and giving me the freedom to share my perspective alongside some of the brightest people in the media industry.

I wouldn't be able to stay afloat without my own immensely talented team: Nick, Parker, Stuart, Sam, Colin, Rob, Daniel, Nar, and Drew. My job is made immeasurably easier knowing that they have my back.

Of course, my family has given me the gift of a lifetime of encouragement and support. I could not be luckier. A special thank-you to Lisa, who helped title this book before a single word of it was written.

Finally, I owe the most gratitude to all those who are doing their part, however big or small, to protect our democracy. When we succeed at preserving this fragile democratic experiment, it will be thanks to the millions of Americans who stayed engaged and informed against all odds. History will remember you.

GOP BRANDING OF NOTE
Donald J. Trump's Eighty-Eight Criminal Counts

(FOR THE HISTORICAL RECORD, LEST YOUR KIDS EVER ASK)

**FIRST INDICTMENT: Stephanie Clifford (a.k.a. "Stormy Daniels")
Hush Money Case**
Charged 3/30/2023; *People of the State of New York v. Donald J. Trump*;
Supreme Court of the State of New York.

COUNTS

1. Falsifying Business Records in the First Degree (N.Y. Penal § 175.10)

2. Falsifying Business Records in the First Degree (N.Y. Penal § 175.10)

3. Falsifying Business Records in the First Degree (N.Y. Penal § 175.10)

4. Falsifying Business Records in the First Degree (N.Y. Penal § 175.10)

5. Falsifying Business Records in the First Degree (N.Y. Penal § 175.10)

6. Falsifying Business Records in the First Degree (N.Y. Penal § 175.10)

7. Falsifying Business Records in the First Degree (N.Y. Penal § 175.10)

8. Falsifying Business Records in the First Degree (N.Y. Penal § 175.10)

9. Falsifying Business Records in the First Degree (N.Y. Penal § 175.10)

10. Falsifying Business Records in the First Degree (N.Y. Penal § 175.10)

11. Falsifying Business Records in the First Degree (N.Y. Penal § 175.10)

12. Falsifying Business Records in the First Degree (N.Y. Penal § 175.10)

13. Falsifying Business Records in the First Degree (N.Y. Penal § 175.10)

14. Falsifying Business Records in the First Degree (N.Y. Penal § 175.10)

15. Falsifying Business Records in the First Degree (N.Y. Penal § 175.10)

16. Falsifying Business Records in the First Degree (N.Y. Penal § 175.10)

17. Falsifying Business Records in the First Degree (N.Y. Penal § 175.10)

18. Falsifying Business Records in the First Degree (N.Y. Penal § 175.10)

19. Falsifying Business Records in the First Degree (N.Y. Penal § 175.10)

20. Falsifying Business Records in the First Degree (N.Y. Penal § 175.10)

21. Falsifying Business Records in the First Degree (N.Y. Penal § 175.10)

22. Falsifying Business Records in the First Degree (N.Y. Penal § 175.10)

23. Falsifying Business Records in the First Degree (N.Y. Penal § 175.10)

24. Falsifying Business Records in the First Degree (N.Y. Penal § 175.10)

25. Falsifying Business Records in the First Degree (N.Y. Penal § 175.10)

26. Falsifying Business Records in the First Degree (N.Y. Penal § 175.10)

27. Falsifying Business Records in the First Degree (N.Y. Penal § 175.10)

28. Falsifying Business Records in the First Degree (N.Y. Penal § 175.10)

29. Falsifying Business Records in the First Degree (N.Y. Penal § 175.10)

30. Falsifying Business Records in the First Degree (N.Y. Penal § 175.10)

31. Falsifying Business Records in the First Degree (N.Y. Penal § 175.10)

32. Falsifying Business Records in the First Degree (N.Y. Penal § 175.10)

33. Falsifying Business Records in the First Degree (N.Y. Penal § 175.10)

34. Falsifying Business Records in the First Degree (N.Y. Penal § 175.10)

SECOND INDICTMENT: **Mar-a-Lago Documents Case**

Charged 06/09/2023; *United States of America v. Donald J. Trump and Waltine Nauta*; United States District Court, Southern District of Florida.

COUNTS

1. Willful Retention of National Defense Information (18 U.S.C. § 793(e))

2. Willful Retention of National Defense Information (18 U.S.C. § 793(e))

3. Willful Retention of National Defense Information (18 U.S.C. § 793(e))

4. Willful Retention of National Defense Information (18 U.S.C. § 793(e))

5. Willful Retention of National Defense Information (18 U.S.C. § 793(e))

6. Willful Retention of National Defense Information (18 U.S.C. § 793(e))

7. Willful Retention of National Defense Information (18 U.S.C. § 793(e))

8. Willful Retention of National Defense Information (18 U.S.C. § 793(e))

9. Willful Retention of National Defense Information (18 U.S.C. § 793(e))

10. Willful Retention of National Defense Information (18 U.S.C. § 793(e))

11. Willful Retention of National Defense Information (18 U.S.C. § 793(e))

12. Willful Retention of National Defense Information (18 U.S.C. § 793(e))

13. Willful Retention of National Defense Information (18 U.S.C. § 793(e))

14. Willful Retention of National Defense Information (18 U.S.C. § 793(e))

15. Willful Retention of National Defense Information (18 U.S.C. § 793(e))

16. Willful Retention of National Defense Information (18 U.S.C. § 793(e))

17. Willful Retention of National Defense Information (18 U.S.C. § 793(e))

18. Willful Retention of National Defense Information (18 U.S.C. § 793(e))

19. Willful Retention of National Defense Information (18 U.S.C. § 793(e))

20. Willful Retention of National Defense Information (18 U.S.C. § 793(e))

21. Willful Retention of National Defense Information (18 U.S.C. § 793(e))

22. Willful Retention of National Defense Information (18 U.S.C. § 793(e))

23. Willful Retention of National Defense Information (18 U.S.C. § 793(e))

24. Willful Retention of National Defense Information (18 U.S.C. § 793(e))

25. Willful Retention of National Defense Information (18 U.S.C. § 793(e))

26. Willful Retention of National Defense Information (18 U.S.C. § 793(e))

27. Willful Retention of National Defense Information (18 U.S.C. § 793(e))

28. Willful Retention of National Defense Information (18 U.S.C. § 793(e))

29. Willful Retention of National Defense Information (18 U.S.C. § 793(e))

30. Willful Retention of National Defense Information (18 U.S.C. § 793(e))

31. Willful Retention of National Defense Information (18 U.S.C. § 793(e))

32. Willful Retention of National Defense Information (18 U.S.C. § 793(e))

33. Conspiracy to Obstruct Justice (18 U.S.C. §1512(k)) [COUNT 33]

34. Withholding a Document or Record (18 U.S.C. §§ 1512(b)(2)(A), 2)

35. Corruptly Concealing a Document or Record (18 U.S.C. §§ 1512(c)(1), 2)

36. Concealing a Document in a Federal Investigation (18 U.S.C. §§ 1519, 2)

37. Scheme to Conceal (18 U.S.C. §§ 1001(a)(1), 2)

SECOND INDICTMENT: **Mar-a-Lago Documents Case, Superseding Indictment**

Charged 07/27/2023; *United States of America v. Donald J. Trump, Waltine Nauta, and Carlos De Oliveira*; United States District Court, Southern District of Florida.

COUNTS

1. False Statements and Representations (18 U.S.C. §§ 1001(a)(2), 2)

2. Altering, Destroying, Mutilating or Concealing an Object (18 U.S.C. §§ 1512(b)(2)(B), 2)

3. Corruptly Altering, Destroying, Mutilating or Concealing a Document, Record, or Other Object (18 U.S.C. §§ 1512(c)(l), 2)

THIRD INDICTMENT: **January 6th Election Obstruction Case**
Charged 08/01/2023; *United States of America v. Donald J. Trump*; District Court for the District of Columbia.

COUNTS

1. Conspiracy to Defraud the United States (18 U.S.C. § 371)

2. Conspiracy to Obstruct an Official Proceeding (18 U.S.C. § 1512(k))

3. Obstruction of and Attempt to Obstruct an Official Proceeding (18 U.S.C. § 1512(c)(2), 2)

4. Conspiracy Against Rights (18 USC § 241)

FOURTH INDICTMENT: **Georgia RICO Election Interference Case**
Charged 08/14/2023; *State of Georgia v. Donald John Trump et al.*; Fulton County Superior Court.

COUNTS

1. Violation of GA RICO (O.C.G.A. § 16-14-4(c))

2. Solicitation of Violation of Oath by Public Officer (O.C.G.A. § 16-4-7 and O.C.G.A. § 16-10-1). *Charge pending further clarification.

3. Conspiracy to Commit Impersonating a Public Officer (O.C.G.A. § 16-4-8 and 16-10-23)

4. Conspiracy to Commit Forgery in the First Degree (O.C.G.A. § 16-4-8 and O.C.G.A. § 16-9-1(b))

5. Conspiracy to Commit False Statements and Writings (O.C.G.A. §§ 16-4-8 and 16-10-20)

6. Conspiracy to Commit Filing False Documents (O.C.G.A. § 16-4-8 and O.C.G.A. § 16-10-20.1(b)(1))

7. Conspiracy to Commit Forgery in the First Degree (O.C.G.A. § 16-4-8 and O.C.G.A. § 16-9-1(b))

8. Conspiracy to Commit Forgery in the First Degree (O.C.G.A. § 16-4-8 and O.C.G.A. § 16-9-1(b))

9. Filing False Documents (O.C.G.A. § 16-10-20.1(b)(1))

10. Solicitation of Violation of Oath by Public Officer (O.C.G.A. § 16-4-7 and O.C.G.A. § 16-10-1). *Charge pending further clarification.

11. False Statements and Writings (O.C.G.A. § 16-10-20)

12. Solicitation of Violation of Oath by Public Officer (O.C.G.A. § 16-4-7 and O.C.G.A. § 16-10-1). *Charge pending further clarification.

13. False Statements and Writings (O.C.G.A. § 16-10-20)

WINNING PRESIDENTIAL SLOGANS

(AND SOME HONORABLE MENTIONS)

1840	William Henry Harrison (Whig)	"Tippecanoe and Tyler Too"
1844	James K. Polk (D)	"54–40 or Fight"
1848	Zachary Taylor (Whig)	"For President of the People"
1852	Franklin Pierce (D)	"We Polked You in '44, We Shall Pierce You in '52"
1856	James Buchanan (D)	"We'll Buck 'em in '56"
1860	Abraham Lincoln (R)	"Vote Yourself a Farm"
1864	Abraham Lincoln (R)	"Don't Swap Horses in Midstream"
1868	Ulysses S. Grant (R)	"Let Us Have Peace"
1872	Ulysses S. Grant (R)	"Grant Us Another Term"
1888	Benjamin Harrison (R)	"Rejuvenated Republicanism"
1896	William McKinley (R)	"Patriotism, Protection, and Prosperity"
1900	William McKinley (R)	"Let Well Enough Alone"
1916	Woodrow Wilson (D)	"He Kept Us Out of War"
1920	Warren G. Harding (R)	"Return to Normalcy"
1924	Calvin Coolidge (R)	"Keep Cool and Keep Coolidge"
1928	Herbert Hoover (R)	"Who but Hoover?"
1932	Franklin D. Roosevelt (D)	"Happy Days Are Here Again"
1936	Franklin D. Roosevelt (D)	"Remember Hoover"

1940	Franklin D. Roosevelt (D)	"Better a Third Term Than a Third Rater"
1944	Franklin D. Roosevelt (D)	"We Are Going to Win This War and the Peace That Follows"
1948	Harry S. Truman (D)	"I'm Just Wild About Harry"
1952	Dwight D. Eisenhower (R)	"I Like Ike"
1956	Dwight D. Eisenhower (R)	"I Still Like Ike"
1960	John F. Kennedy (D)	"A Time for Greatness"
1964	Lyndon B. Johnson (D)	"All the Way with LBJ"
1968	Richard Nixon (R)	"This Time, Vote Like Your Whole World Depended on It"
1972	Richard Nixon (R)	"President Nixon. Now More Than Ever"
1976	Jimmy Carter (D)	"A Leader, for a Change"
1980	Ronald Reagan (R)	"Are You Better Off Than You Were Four Years Ago?"
1984	Ronald Reagan (R)	"It's Morning Again in America"
1988	George Bush (R)	"Kinder, Gentler Nation"
1992	Bill Clinton (D)	"For People, for a Change"
1996	Bill Clinton (D)	"Building a Bridge to the 21st Century"
2000	George W. Bush (R)	"A Reformer with Results"
2004	George W. Bush (R)	"Building a Safer World and a More Hopeful America"
2008	Barack Obama (D)	"Change We Can Believe In"
2012	Barack Obama (D)	"Forward"
2016	Donald J. Trump (R)	"Make America Great Again"
2020	Joseph R. Biden (D)	"Restore the Soul of the Nation"
2024	Donald Trump (R)	"I Was Indicted for You!"
2024	Joseph R. Biden (D)	"Let's Finish the Job"

HONORABLE MENTIONS (USED OFFICIALLY OR BY CAMPAIGNS)

1844	Henry Clay (Whig)	"Who Is James K. Polk?"
1868	Ulysses. S. Grant (R)	"Vote as You Shoot"
1884	James G. Blaine (R)	"Ma, Ma, Where's My Pa?" (used by supporters against Grover Cleveland, who had allegedly fathered an illegitimate child)
1884	Grover Cleveland (D)	"Blaine, Blaine, James G. Blaine! The Continental Liar from the State of Maine!"
1888	Benjamin Harrison (R)	"Grandfather's Hat Fits Ben!" (referring to William Henry Harrison)
1896	William Jennings Bryan (D)	"No Cross of Gold, No Crown of Thorns"
1900	William McKinley (R)	"Four More Years of the Full Dinner Pail"
1900	William Howard Taft (D)	"Vote for Taft Now, You Can Vote for Bryan Any Time"
1912	William Howard Taft (D)	"It Is Nothing but Fair to Leave Taft in the Chair"
1912	Woodrow Wilson (D)	"Vote for 8 Hour Wilson"
1916	Woodrow Wilson (D)	"He Proved the Pen Mightier than the Sword"
1916	Woodrow Wilson (D)	"War in the East, Peace in the West, Thank God for Woodrow Wilson"
1920	Eugene V. Debs (Socialist)	"From Atlanta Prison to the White House"
1928	Al Smith (D)	"Make Your Wet Dreams Come True" (his stand for repealing Prohibition)
1936	Alfred M. Landon (R)	"Let's Make It a Landon-Slide"
1944	Thomas E. Dewey (R)	"Dewey or Don't We"
1948	Harry S. Truman (D)	"Pour It on 'em, Harry!"

1956	Adlai Stevenson (D)	"Adlai and Estes—The Bestest" (Adlai Stevenson and Estes Kefauver)
1964	Barry Goldwater (R)	"In Your Heart, You Know He's Right"
1964	Lyndon B. Johnson (D)	"In Your Guts, You Know He's Nuts" (in response)
1972	Richard M. Nixon (R)	"Don't Change Dicks in the Midst of a Screw, Vote for Nixon in '72"
1976	Jimmy Carter (D)	"Not Just Peanuts"
1976	Jimmy Carter (Georgia) and Walter Mondale (Minnesota) (D)	"Peaches and Cream"
1980	Ronald Reagan (R)	"Let's Make America Great Again"
1980	Walter Mondale (D)	"Where's the Beef?"
1988	George H. W. Bush (R)	"Read My Lips, No New Taxes"
1992	George H. W. Bush (R)	"Don't Change the Team in the Middle of the Stream"
1992	Pat Buchanan (R)	"Down with King George" (in reference to Bush)
1992	Ross Perot (I)	"I'm Ross, and You're the Boss!"
1996	Pat Buchanan (D)	"Go Pat Go"
2016	Lindsey Graham (R)	"Ready to be Commander in Chief on Day One"
2016	Bobby Jindal (R)	"Tanned, Rested, Ready"
2016	Rand Paul (R)	"Defeat the Washington Machine. Unleash the American Dream."
2020	Joseph R. Biden (D)	"No Malarkey!"
2020	Bernie Sanders (D)	"Feel the Bern"
2020	Michael Bloomberg (D)	"I Like Mike"
2020	John McAfee (L)	"Don't Vote McAfee"
2024	Mike Pence (R)	"I Like Mike"

NOTES

PROLOGUE: Chaos in the Chamber

2 Gaetz was photographed: Howard Koplowitz, "Mike Rogers Restrained in Angry Confrontation with Matt Gaetz over Speaker Vote," AL.com, January 6, 2023, updated January 7, 2023, https://www.al.com/politics/2023/01/mike-rogers-restrained-in-angry-confrontation-with-matt-gaetz-over-speaker-vote.html.

CHAPTER 1: The Road to Shamelessness

11 Sheldon Whitehouse describes: Sheldon Whitehouse, Speeches: "The Scheme 1: The Powell Memo," May 27, 2021, https://www.whitehouse.senate.gov/news/speeches/the-scheme-1-the-powell-memo/.

11 "No thoughtful person can question": Lewis F. Powell Jr., "Attack on American Free Enterprise System," memo to Eugene B. Sydnor Jr., chairman, Education Committee, U.S. Chamber of Commerce, August 23, 1971, https://scholarlycommons.law.wlu.edu/cgi/viewcontent.cgi?article=1000&context=powellmemo.

12 "the ultimate issue may be survival": Ibid.

13 "Government is not the solution": Ronald Reagan, Reagan Quotes & Speeches, Inaugural Address, January 20, 1981, https://www.reaganfoundation.org/ronald-reagan/reagan-quotes-speeches/inaugural-address-2/.

14 "name-calling, conspiracy theories": McKay Coppins, "The Man Who Broke Politics," *The Atlantic*, updated October 17, 2018, https://www.theatlantic.com/magazine/archive/2018/11 /newt-gingrich-says-youre-welcome/570832/.

15 "learn to 'raise hell'": Ibid.

15 Lilliana Mason identified: Lilliana Mason, *Uncivil Agreement: How Politics Became Our Identity* (Chicago: University of Chicago Press, 2018), https://press.uchicago.edu/ucp/books/book/chicago/U /bo27527354.html.

16 "run for public office": Jan Crawford, "Gingrich Surging, but Faces Tough Questions," CBS News, January 20, 2012, https://www .cbsnews.com/news/gingrich-surging-but-faces-tough-questions/.

17 "A Plan for Putting the GOP": John Cook, "Roger Ailes' Secret Nixon-Era Blueprint for Fox News Revealed," *Gawker*, June 30, 2011, available at Benton Institute for Broadband & Society, https://www.benton.org/headlines/roger-ailes%E2%80%99 -secret-nixon-era-blueprint-fox-news. See also https://www .documentcloud.org/documents/5024551-A-Plan-for -Putting-the-GOP-on-the-News.

18 Republicans introduced Project REDMAP: Lee Drutman, "Where We Have Been: The History of Gerrymandering in America," *What We Know About Redistricting and Redistricting Reform*, New America, updated September 19, 2022, https://www.newamerica .org/political-reform/reports/what-we-know-about-redistricting -and-redistricting-reform/where-we-have-been-the-history -of-gerrymandering-in-america/.

CHAPTER 2: **Labels and Lies**

31 at least twenty-six women: Eliza Relman and Azmi Haroun, "The 26 Women Who Have Accused Trump of Sexual Misconduct," *Business Insider*, updated May 9, 2023, https://www.businessinsider.com /women-accused-trump-sexual-misconduct-list-2017-12.

31   Lewis A. Kaplan elucidated: Martin Pengelly, "Judge Says E. Jean
      Carroll Allegation Trump Raped Her Is 'Substantially True' in Court
      Dismissal," *Guardian*, August 7, 2023, https://www.theguardian.com
      /us-news/2023/aug/07/donald-trump-rape-language-e-jean-carroll.

32   Donald allegedly had an affair: Kate Taylor and Erin Snodgrass,
      "A Timeline of Donald Trump's Three Marriages, Numerous
      Rumored Affairs, and Sexual Misconduct Allegations," *Business
      Insider*, April 4, 2023, https://www.businessinsider.com/trump
      -melania-stormy-daniels-affairs-marriages-timeline-2018-3.

32   Sessions shamelessly admitted: "Sessions Admits Policy Is a
      Deterrent," CNN Politics, June 19, 2018, https://www.cnn.com
      /videos/politics/2018/06/19/sessions-defends-controversial
      -immigration-policy-deterrent-sot.cnn.

33   recall using campaign funds: Nicholas Fandos, "How Santos Spent
      Donors' Money: Ferragamo, OnlyFans and Botox," *New York Times*,
      November 16, 2023, updated November 29, 2023, https://www
      .nytimes.com/2023/11/16/nyregion/santos-botox-ferragamo-expenses
      .html.

34   "bizarre choices," Johnson wrote: Andrew Kaczynski and Allison
      Gordon, "New Speaker of the House Mike Johnson Once Wrote
      in Support of the Criminalization of Gay Sex," CNN Politics,
      October 27, 2023, https://www.cnn.com/2023/10/25/politics
      /mike-johnson-gay-sex-criminalization-kfile/index.html.

34   "accountability partner": Daniel Kreps, "Mike Johnson Admits
      He and His Son Monitor Each Other's Porn Intake in Resurfaced
      Video," *Rolling Stone*, November 5, 2023, https://www.rollingstone
      .com/politics/politics-news/mike-johnson-son-monitor-porn-intake
      -covenant-eyes-1234870634/.

35   child labor laws: Timothy Noah, "Umm, GOP: When Did
      You Become the Pro–Child Labor Party?," *The New Republic*,
      October 23, 2023, https://newrepublic.com/article/176373/gop
      -pro-child-labor-party.

35   life-saving health care: Tori Otten, "Alabama Judges Use Abortion Ban Logic to Block Care for Trans Minors," *The New Republic*, August 21, 2023, https://newrepublic.com/post/175112 /alabama-judges-use-abortion-ban-logic-block-care-trans-minors.

35   ban free school lunches: Prem Thakker, "Republicans Declare Banning Universal Free School Meals a 2024 Priority," *The New Republic*, June 15, 2023, https://newrepublic.com/post/173668 /republicans-declare-banning-universal-free-school-meals-2024 -priority.

35   getting "good vibes": "THUNE TAX VIBE CHECK" (@ReporterCioffi, December 13, 2022), https://twitter.com /ReporterCioffi/status/1602703762858049540.

36   upholding "fiscal responsibility": "State Fact Sheets: House Republicans' Funding Bills Would Have Devastating Impacts for Hard-Working Families Across America," White House, September 12, 2023, https://www.whitehouse.gov/briefing-room /statements-releases/2023/09/12/state-fact-sheets-house-republicans -funding-bills-would-have-devastating-impacts-for-hard-working -families-across-america/.

37   interview with Bob Woodward: Bob Woodward and Robert Costa, "Transcript: Donald Trump Interview with Bob Woodward and Robert Costa," *Washington Post*, April 2, 2016, https://www .washingtonpost.com/news/post-politics/wp/2016/04/02 /transcript-donald-trump-interview-with-bob-woodward-and -robert-costa/.

38   passed by 95 percent: K. K. Rebecca Lai, Wilson Andrews, and Alicia Parlapiano, "How Every Member Voted on the House Tax Bill," *New York Times*, November 16, 2017, https://www.nytimes .com/interactive/2017/11/16/us/politics/house-vote-republican -tax-bill.html.

38   by $7.8 trillion: Allan Sloan and Cezary Podkul, "Donald Trump Built a National Debt So Big (Even Before the Pandemic) That

It'll Weigh Down the Economy for Years," ProPublica, January 14, 2021, https://www.propublica.org/article/national-debt-trump.

39   wealthiest Americans paid: Christopher Ingraham, "For the First Time in History, U.S. Billionaires Paid a Lower Tax Rate Than the Working Class Last Year," *Washington Post*, October 8, 2019, https://www.washingtonpost.com/business/2019/10/08/first-time-history-us-billionaires-paid-lower-tax-rate-than-working-class-last-year/.

39   promised "a return": Ken Tran, "Mike Johnson Reveals House GOP Agenda in First Press Conference as Speaker: What You Missed," *USA Today*, November 2, 2023, https://www.usatoday.com/story/news/politics/2023/11/02/mike-johnson-israel-government-shutdown-ukraine-impeachment/714422813007/.

39   IRS was clear: Jacob Bogage and Jeff Stein, "GOP Plan to Fund Israel Aid with IRS Cuts Would Cost $90 Billion, Tax Chief Says," *Washington Post*, November 1, 2023, https://www.washingtonpost.com/business/2023/11/01/israel-aid-irs-gop/.

40   This process had played: "Debt Limit," U.S. Department of the Treasury, n.d., https://home.treasury.gov/policy-issues/financial-markets-financial-institutions-and-fiscal-service/debt-limit.

42   Chip Roy tweeted: "Today, a number of my colleagues will be filing an amicus brief in support of the lawsuit filed by the State of Texas regarding the election results of several other states . . ." (@chiproytx, December 10, 2020), https://twitter.com/chiproytx/status/1337090007937527811.

42   John Cornyn said: Aaron Blake, "Can Trump's Lawyers Get in Trouble for Frivolous Lawsuits?," *Washington Post*, December 11, 2020, https://www.washingtonpost.com/politics/2020/12/11/can-trumps-lawyers-get-trouble-frivolous-lawsuits/.

42   Chris Smith introduced: Maggie Jo Buchanan, "What You Need to Know About the Bill to Ban Abortion Nationwide," American Progress, September 16, 2022, https://www.americanprogress.org

/article/what-you-need-to-know-about-the-bill-to-ban-abortion
-nationwide/.

43 opted to enshrine those rights: Julie Carr Smyth, "Ohio
    Voters Enshrine Abortion Access in Constitution in Latest
    Statewide Win for Reproductive Rights," Associated Press,
    November 7, 2023, https://apnews.com/article/ohio-abortion
    -amendment-election-2023-fe3e06747b616507d8ca21ea26485270.

44 "This sweeping hole": Nick Schifrin, "Tuberville's Hold on
    Military Promotions Is Impacting Troop Readiness, Mullen Says,"
    PBS NewsHour, August 22, 2023, https://www.pbs.org/newshour
    /show/tubervilles-hold-on-military-promotions-is-impacting
    -troop-readiness-mullen-says.

45 "I like people that weren't captured": Calvin Woodward and Hope
    Yen, "AP Fact Check: Trump on McCain . . .," NPR, September 5,
    2020, https://www.pbs.org/newshour/nation/__trashed-2.

46 "Congress members . . . whom I had guarded": Harry Dunn,
    Standing My Ground (New York: Hachette, 2023), 93.

46 in the days and months after: https://www.reuters.com/world
    /us/officer-who-responded-us-capitol-attack-is-third-die-by
    -suicide-2021-08-02/; https://www.factcheck.org/2021/11
    /how-many-died-as-a-result-of-capitol-riot/.

47 $10 billion of which was committed: Justin Gomez, "Biden to
    Announce $10 Billion from American Rescue Plan for Policing,
    Public Safety," ABC News, May 13, 2022, https://abcnews.go.com
    /Politics/biden-announce-10-billion-american-rescue-plan-policing
    /story?id=84685199.

47 House Republicans threatened: Chris Pandolfo, "Texas
    Republicans Call on House to Defund DHS If Biden Won't Secure
    the Border," Fox News, August 10, 2023, https://luttrell.house
    .gov/media/in-the-news/texas-republicans-call-house-defund-dhs
    -if-biden-wont-secure-border-0.

48   "If Steve Bannon and I": Zach Williams, "Marjorie Taylor Greene
       and Donald Trump Jr. Dash Dems at NY Young
       Republican Gala," *New York Post*, December 11, 2022,
       updated December 28, 2022, https://nypost.com/2022/12/11
       /marjorie-taylor-greene-donald-trump-jr-bash-dems-at-gop-gala/.

48   "It will be my honor": "My Statements on Being Assigned to the
       House Committee on Oversight and Accountability and the House
       Committee on Homeland Security for the 118th Congress"
       (@RepMTG, January 17, 2023), https://twitter.com/RepMTG
       /status/1615493790793609217.

51   Nothing less than a miracle: Ronald Reagan, "Inaugural Address
       1981," Ronald Reagan Presidential Library & Museum, January
       20, 1981, https://www.reaganlibrary.gov/archives/speech/
       inaugural-address-1981.

52   terminating the Constitution: Hope Yen, "Trump Rebuked for
       Call to Suspend Constitution over Election," Associated Press,
       December 4, 2022, https://apnews.com/article/social-media
       -donald-trump-8e6e2f0a092135428c82c0cfa6598444.

52   "a dictator" on "day one": Jill Colvin and Bill Barrow, "Trump's
       Vow to Only Be a Dictator on 'Day One' Follows Growing Worry
       over His Authoritarian Rhetoric," Associated Press, December 7,
       2023, https://apnews.com/article/trump-hannity-dictator
       -authoritarian-presidential-election-f27e7e9d7c13fabbe3ae7dd7f1
       235c72.

53   appetites of one man: President Joe Biden, "Remarks by
       President Biden on the Third Anniversary of the January 6th
       Attack and Defending the Sacred Cause of American Democracy |
       Blue Bell, PA," White House, January 6, 2024, https://www
       .whitehouse.gov/briefing-room/speeches-remarks/2024/01/05
       /remarks-by-president-biden-on-the-third-anniversary-of-the
       -january-6th-attack-and-defending-the-sacred-cause-of-american
       -democracy-blue-bell-pa/.

CHAPTER 3: **The Post-Hypocrisy Party**

55   the Lincoln Project put out an ad: "Flip Flop Lindsey," The Lincoln Project, YouTube video, January 13, 2022, https://www .youtube.com/watch?v=panBlLiPgfA.

57   "Fellow Americans beat": "Read McConnell's Remarks on the Senate Floor Following Trump's Acquittal," CNN Politics, February 13, 2021, https://cnn.com/2021/02/13/politics /mcconnell-remarks-trump-acquittal/index.html.

58   calling out McConnell's shameless hypocrisy: Jennifer Rubin, "This Is How Bad McConnell Really Is," *Washington Post*, February 14, 2021, https://www.washingtonpost.com/opinions/2021/02/14 /this-is-how-bad-mcconnell-really-is/.

58   "The founders of this country": Ewan Palmer, "Mike Johnson's Words Come Back to Haunt Him," *Newsweek*, December 13, 2023, https://www.newsweek.com/ mike-johnson-joe-biden-impeachment-vote-gop-1851927.

59   "If you don't like the president": Andrew Kaczynski and Em Steck, "House Speaker Mike Johnson Pursues Impeachment Strategy He Once Said Could Cause 'Irreparable Damage' to the Country," CNN Politics, December 11, 2023, https://www.cnn .com/2023/12/11/politics/kfile-johnson-impeachment-strategy -irreparable-damage-invs/index.html.

60   "What is the specific constitutional crime that you are inves- tigating?": Aaron Blake, "A Revealing Exchange on the GOP's Speculative Impeachment inquiry," *Washington Post*, December 12, 2003, https://www.washingtonpost.com/politics/2023/12/13 /republican-impeachment-case-analysis/.

60   "have not connected the dots": "Fox host: The Republicans at this point don't have—they have not connected the dots. They have not shown where Joe Biden did anything illegally"

(@Biden-Harris HQ, December 11, 2023), https://twitter.com/BidenHQ/status/1734252990431641732?s=20.

62   "It doesn't change the fundamental": "Judiciary Committee Chair Jim Jordan on Biden Investigation and Alexander Smirnov Indictment," C-SPAN, February 21, 2024, https://www.c-span.org/video/?533716-101/judiciary-committee-chair-jim-jordan-biden-investigation-alexander-smirnov-indictment.

63   "madcap wild goose chase": Lucy Strathmore, "U.S. Congressman Burns Marjorie Taylor Greene, Too Good Not to Share," MSN, February 6, 2024, https://www.msn.com/en-us/news/politics/u-s-congressman-burns-marjorie-taylor-greene-too-good-not-to-share/ar-BB1hVJYw.

69   "I actually think this flips": Brian Tyler Cohen, "Top Senator Calls Out Glaring Republican Failures on the Border," *Interviews with Brian Tyler Cohen*, YouTube video, February 11, 2024, https://www.youtube.com/watch?v=gMjZxsJNRtE.

76   "perfect" phone call: Caroline Vakil, "Trump Defends 'Perfect' Call with Raffensperger amid Threat of Prison Sentences from Georgia Probe," *The Hill*, September 19, 2022, https://thehill.com/homenews/campaign/3651039-trump-defends-perfect-call-with-raffensperger-amid-threat-of-prison-sentences-from-georgia-probe/.

80   "greedy for our country": Conor Lynch, "Donald Trump's Creed of Greed: Product of a Society That Puts Profit Before People," Salon, April 28, 2018, https://www.salon.com/2018/04/28/donald-trumps-creed-of-greed-product-of-a-society-that-puts-profit-before-people/.

80   He told over thirty thousand lies: Glenn Kessler, Salvador Rizzo, and Meg Kelly, "Trump's False or Misleading Claims Total 30,573 over 4 Years," *Washington Post*, January 24, 2021, https://www.washingtonpost.com/politics/2021/01/24/trumps-false-or-misleading-claims-total-30573-over-four-years/.

CHAPTER 4: **Continued on Next Bumper Sticker**

82   Betsy Reed dubbed the "ideas primary": Lauren Gambino, "'I Have a Plan for That': Elizabeth Warren Leads the Democratic 'Ideas Primary,'" *Guardian*, May 11, 2019, https://www.theguardian.com/us-news/2019/may/11/i-have-a-plan-for-that-elizabeth-warren-democratic-policy-primary.

84   "Conventional wisdom is": Jon Stewart, "Talking Points," *The Daily Show*, Comedy Central, July 15, 2004, https://www.cc.com/video/dkt5k4/the-daily-show-with-jon-stewart-talking-points.

86   "An Orwellian label": Gregg Easterbrook, "Clear Skies, No Lies," Brookings Institution, February 16, 2005, https://www.brookings.edu/articles/clear-skies-no-lies/.

90   "We are a bigger, broader coalition": Brian Tyler Cohen, "Al Franken on Whether Trump Officials Should Be Punished," *Interviews with Brian Tyler Cohen*, YouTube video, December 21, 2020, https://www.youtube.com/watch?v=PhrMUxO4hxE.

91   White voters made up 87 percent: Pew Research Center, "Demographic Profiles of Republican and Democratic Voters," Pew Research, July 12, 2023, https://www.pewresearch.org/politics/2023/07/12/demographic-profiles-of-republican-and-democratic-voters/.

91   more than four hundred: Adam Gabbatt, "Fox News Suddenly Goes Quiet on 'Great Replacement' Theory After Buffalo Shooting," *Guardian*, May 17, 2022, https://www.theguardian.com/us-news/2022/may/17/buffalo-shooting-fox-news-tucker-carlson-great-replacement-theory.

91   "over the final two weeks": Philip Bump, "The Caravan Has All but Vanished from Cable News," *Washington Post*, November 9, 2018, https://www.washingtonpost.com/politics/2018/11/09/caravan-has-all-vanished-cable-news/.

92 Mitt Romney's 44-point: Seung Min Kim, "Senate Passes Immigration Bill," *Politico*, June 27, 2013, https://www.politico .com/story/2013/06/immigration-bill-2013-senate-passes-093530.

93 "comms rather than legislation": Abby Vesoulis, "Why Madison Cawthorn Lost His Race," *Time*, May 18, 2022, https://time.com /6178176/madison-cawthorn-lost-north-carolina/.

94 "flood[ing] the zone with shit": Michael Lewis, "Has Anyone Seen the President?," Bloomberg, February 9, 2018, https://www.bloomberg.com/view/articles/2018-02-09/ has-anyone-seen-the-president.

94 a deluge of witness depositions: House Oversight and Accountability, 118th Congress, "The Basis for an Impeachment Inquiry of President Joseph R. Biden, Jr.," Congress.Gov, September 28, 2023, https://www.congress.gov/event /118th-congress/house-event/LC71519/text?s=1&r=37.

95 Steve Doocy admitted: "Steve Doocy on Fox & Friends: 'Republicans do not have enough votes to impeach. And after dozens of interviews and over 100,000 documents released, Republicans have yet to produce any direct evidence of misconduct by Biden'" (@atrupar, February 28, 2024), https://twitter.com /atrupar/status/1762943609433649182?s=20.

95 Obama himself conceded: Andrew Kaczynski, "Obama Says the Administration 'Didn't Make a Hard Sell' for Obamacare," BuzzFeed News, April 1, 2014, https://www.buzzfeednews.com /article/andrewkaczynski/obama-says-the-administration- didnt-make-a-hard-sell-for-oba.

98 "election interference witch hunt": (@realDonaldTrump, October 17, 2023), https://truthsocial.com/@realDonaldTrump /posts/111251425911489751.

98 nearly three-quarters of Republicans believed: Filip Timotija, "Most Republicans in New Poll Believe Trump's Legal Cases Are

Being Handled 'Unfairly,'" *The Hill*, February 3, 2024, https://thehill.com/regulation/court-battles/4446963-most-republicans-believe-trump-legal-cases-handled-unfairly/.

CHAPTER 5: Man Bites Dog

101   "Of course, just what is threatening democracy": Jonathan Weisman, "Fears over Fate of Democracy Leave Many Voters Frustrated and Resigned," *New York Times*, October 23, 2022, https://www.nytimes.com/2022/10/23/us/politics/voting-democracy-wisconsin-senate.html.

103   who, it was revealed: Olivia Nuzzi, "Donald Trump and Sean Hannity Like to Talk Before Bedtime," *New York Magazine*, May 2018, https://nymag.com/intelligencer/2018/05/sean-hannity-donald-trump-late-night-calls.html.

103   opportunity "to decompress": Ibid.

103   at a rally: David Bauder, "Fox's Hannity Speaks Onstage at Trump Campaign Rally," Associated Press, November 6, 2018, https://apnews.com/article/20f240baf06742c79de711d7e8580eb9.

104   a fake *Time* magazine: David A. Fahrenthold, "A Time Magazine with Trump on the Cover Hangs in His Golf Clubs. It's Fake," June 27, 2017, https://www.washingtonpost.com/politics/a-time-magazine-with-trump-on-the-cover-hangs-in-his-golf-clubs-its-fake/2017/06/27/0adf96de-5850-11e7-ba90-f5875b7d1876_story.html.

105   "In just six days": Duncan J. Watts and David M. Rothschild, "Don't Blame the Election on Fake News. Blame It on the Media," *Columbia Journalism Review*, December 5, 2017, https://www.cjr.org/analysis/fake-news-media-election-trump.php.

107   "Everybody thought that Hillary Clinton": "Kevin McCarthy: Benghazi Committee Tanked Hillary's Poll Numbers," FoxNews clip posted by Talking Points Memo TV, YouTube video,

September 30, 2015, https://www.youtube.com
/watch?v=x8Wff2-IKkA.

107 "All I can say is": Nikki McCann Ramírez, "GOP Rep. Explains
Impeachment Push," *Rolling Stone*, December 13, 2023, https://
www.rollingstone.com/politics/politics-news/troy-nehls-biden
-impeachment-inquiry-donald-trump-2024-1234927472/.

112 "Most Republicans agree": Kabir Khana, "CBS News Analysis:
Most Republicans Agree with 'Poisoning the Blood' Language,"
CBS News, January 14, 2024, https://www.cbsnews.com/news/
cbs-news-analysis-most-republicans-agree-with-poisoning-the-
blood-language/.

112 "Tuberville backs Trump's": Mark Satter, "Tuberville
Backs Trump's 'Poisoning the Blood' Rhetoric," *Roll Call*,
December 19, 2023, https://rollcall.com/2023/12/19/
tuberville-backs-trumps-poisoning-the-blood-rhetoric/.

112 "'Well, it's not hateful'": Miranda Nazzaro, "Johnson Defends
Trump's 'Poisoning' Immigrant Remark: 'It's Not Hateful,'"
The Hill, January 7, 2024, https://thehill.com/homenews
/house/4393941-johnson-defends-trumps-poisoning-immigrant
-remark-its-not-hateful/.

114 "Which Is Worse": Patrick Healy, "Which Is Worse: Biden's Age or
Trump Handing NATO to Putin?," *New York Times*, February 12,
2024, https://www.nytimes.com/live/2024/02/06/opinion
/thepoint#biden-age-trump-nato.

114 "The 2024 Campaign Gets Grimmer": Stephen Collinson, "The
2024 Campaign Gets Grimmer, with Trump's Extremism on Full
Display Alongside Concerns over Biden's Age," CNN, February 12,
2024, https://www.cnn.com/2024/02/12/politics/trump-biden
-election-2024/index.html.

115 "largest domestic deportation operation": Isaac Arnsdorf, Nick
Miroff, and Josh Dawsey, "Trump and Allies Planning Militarized

Mass Deportations, Detention Camps," *Washington Post*, February 21, 2024, https://www.washingtonpost.com/politics/2024/02/20 /trump-mass-deportations-immigration/.

117 "We know that he": "Obama Slams Trump over 'Secret' Chinese Bank Account," Reuters, YouTube video, October 21, 2020, https://www.youtube.com/watch?v=m8LcPRoClMA.

117 Fox News ran: Brandon Gillespie, "Hunter Biden Faces Backlash After Defying Subpoena with Press Conference 'Stunt,'" Fox News, December 13, 2023, https://www.foxnews.com/politics/hunter -biden-faces-backlash-defying-subpoena-press-conference-stunt -contempt.

117 approving a contempt resolution: Alexandra Hutzler and Lauren Peller, "GOP-Led Committees Approve Contempt Resolution Against Hunter Biden, Will Subpoena Him Again," ABC News, January 14, 2024, https://abcnews.go.com/Politics /house-republicans-push-vote-holding-hunter-biden-contempt /story?id=106223828.

118 Hunter Biden in contempt: House Judiciary, "Resolution Recommending That the House of Representatives Find Robert Hunter Biden in Contempt of Congress for Refusal to Comply with a Subpoena Duly Issued by the Committee on the Judiciary," January 2024, https://judiciary.house.gov/sites/evo-subsites /republicans-judiciary.house.gov/files/evo-media-document /hunter-biden-contempt-report.pdf.

118 "How Biden's Immigration Fight": Zolan Kanno-Youngs and Erica L. Green, "How Biden's Immigration Fight Threatens His Biggest Foreign Policy Win," *New York Times*, January 19, 2024, https://www.nytimes.com/2024/01/19/us/politics/biden -immigration-ukraine.html.

119 "A Border Deal now would": Alexander Ward and Matt Berg, "World Court Ruling Tests a Core Biden Claim," *Politico*,

January 26, 2024, https://www.politico.com/newsletters
/national-security-daily/2024/01/26/world-court-ruling-tests
-a-core-biden-claim-00137932.

119   "Why would I?": Manu Raju, Melanie Zanona, and Lauren Fox,
       "A Border Deal to Nowhere? House GOP Ready to Reject Senate
       Compromise on Immigration," CNN Politics, January 3, 2024,
       https://www.cnn.com/2024/01/03/politics/senate-immigration
       -negotiations-congress/index.html.

120   "There is absolutely no": "Ingraham: Senator, is this deal dead
       effectively? Hawley: I hope so. There is no reason to agree to
       policies that would further enable Joe Biden" (@Acyn, January 25,
       2024), https://twitter.com/Acyn/status/1750676533511
       921847.

120   "We don't want to do": Jake Sherman and Laura Weiss, "What
       McConnell's Border Play Means," *Punchbowl News*, January 25,
       2024, https://punchbowl.news/archive/12524-punchbowl
       -news-am.

120   Secure the Border Act: Ted Cruz Press Release, "Senator Cruz
       Introduces Comprehensive Border Security Amendment to the
       National Security Supplemental," December 12, 2023, https://
       www.cruz.senate.gov/newsroom/press-releases/sen-cruz-introduces
       -comprehensive-border-security-amendment-to-the-national-security
       -supplemental.

120   grilled Senator James Lankford: "Fox News: Why give Biden this in
       an election year? He gets to take a victory lap" (@atrupar, January 28,
       2024), https://twitter.com/atrupar/status/1751621658513637866?
       s=10&t=T33hxNllTQ7uyBaIkC-PIg.

120   "I had a popular commentator": "Sen. Lankford reveals threat he
       received from a popular commentator over border bill" (@CNN,
       February 7, 2024), YouTube Short, https://www.youtube.com
       /shorts/E4EVoMTCtVM.

CHAPTER 6: **If You Build It . . .**

123   "funding father of the conservative movement": Jeffrey H. Birnbaum, "Liberal Praise Drawn from Unlikely Source," *Washington Post*, October 18, 2004, http:/www.washingtonpost .com/ac2/wp-dyn/A40634-2004Oct17?language=printer.

123   "build support for 'New Right'": Ibid.

123   "Strength lies in organization": Powell Jr., "Attack on American Free Enterprise System."

124   "single most important requirement": "Fairness Doctrine," Ronald Reagan Presidential Library & Museum, last updated April 7, 2023, https://www.reaganlibrary.gov/archives/topic-guide /fairness-doctrine.

124   "wrong-headed, misguided, and illogical": Robert D. Hershey Jr., *New York Times*, August 5, 1987, https://www.nytimes.com /1987/08/05/arts/fcc-votes-down-fairness-doctrine-in-a-4-0 -decision.html.

125   "conservative-media revolution": Rush Limbaugh, "The Conservative-Media Revolution Has Forced the Liberal Media to Abandon Any Pretense of Objectivity," *National Review*, November 4, 2015, https://www.nationalreview.com/2015/11 /rush-limbaugh-national-review-conservative-media-revolution/.

125   "the Number One voice for conservatism": David Remnick, "Day of the Dittohead," *Washington Post*, February 20, 1994, https://www.washingtonpost.com/archive/opinions/1994/02/20 /day-of-the-dittohead/e5723f05-04d8-4ccb-98c9-8b1ba6c358d2/.

125   "Feminism was established": Anthony Zurcher, "Rush Limbaugh: How He Used Shock to Reshape America," BBC.com, February 17, 2021, https://www.bbc.com/news/world-us-canada-56105331; *60 Minutes Overtime*, 1991, (@60minutes, February 5, 2020) Instagram post, https://www.instagram.com/p/B8Mw1dgBSf4/.

125   "I think it's time to get rid of": Andrew Seifter, "Limbaugh on
      the NBA: 'Call It the TBA, the Thug Basketball Association . . .
      They're Going in to Watch the Crips and the Bloods,'" Media
      Matters for America, December 10, 2004, https://www.media
      matters.org/rush-limbaugh/limbaugh-nba-call-it-tba-thug
      -basketball-association-theyre-going-watch-crips-and.

125   "If any race of people": Clare Kim, "'White Guilt'? Forget It:
      Whites Have 'Done More to End' Slavery Than 'Any Other Race,'
      Says Rush Limbaugh," NBC News, July 22, 2013, https://www
      .nbcnews.com/id/wbna52550027.

125   "When a gay person": Morgan Whitaker, "Rush Limbaugh's 25
      Most Outrageous Moments in 25 Years on the Radio," NBC News,
      July 31, 2013, https://www.nbcnews.com/id/wbna52638222.

125   Limbaugh began airing: David Ehrenstein, "Obama the 'Magic
      Negro,'" *Los Angeles Times*, March 19, 2007, https://www.latimes
      .com/la-oe-ehrenstein19mar19-story.html.

126   more than 88.8 million: Shane Croucher and Jacob Jarvis,
      "Who's the Top MAGA Influencer Six Months After Trump Social
      Media Ban?," *Newsweek*, July 6, 2021, https://www.newsweek
      .com/2021/07/09/20-most-influential-trump-supporters-survive
      -social-medias-capitol-riot-crackdown-1606525.html.

127   according to the Daily Beast: Jake Lahut and Zachary Petrizzo,
      "Trail Mix: Trump Tries to Beat DeSantis at Influencer Game,"
      Daily Beast, March 24, 2023, updated December 15, 2023,
      https://www.thedailybeast.com/trail-mix-trump-woos-maga
      -influencers-posobiec-raichik-and-fournier-at-mar-a-lago.

128   "It is everything": Anthony Zurcher, "Rush Limbaugh: How He
      Used Shock to Reshape America," BBC.com, February 17, 2021,
      https://www.bbc.com/news/world-us-canada-56105331.

129   "Republicans just bought this conservative-backed": "Mehdi
      Hasan and Jon Favreau React to Joe Biden's Town Hall," *Pod Save*

America, YouTube video, July 22, 2021, https://www.youtube.com /watch?v=dzc_NWaqwwA.

130   "Americans Know": Aaron Blake, "Americans Know Trump Is Extreme. They Might Elect Him Anyway," *Washington Post*, February 5, 2024, https://www.washingtonpost.com/politics/2024/02/05/americans -know-trump-is-extreme-they-might-elect-him-anyway/.

130   "Republicans Now Say": Aaron Blake, "Americans Now Say It Might Be Okay to Ignore the Supreme Court," *Washington Post*, January 29, 2024, https://www.washingtonpost .com/politics/2024/01/29/republicans-now-say-it-might- be-okay-ignore-supreme-court/.

131   "With both far-right and hard-left": Catie Edmondson, "House Passes Debt Limit Bill in Bipartisan Vote to Avert Default," *New York Times*, May 31, 2023, updated June 2, 2023, https://www .nytimes.com/2023/05/31/us/politics/debt-ceiling-house-vote.html.

132   Sean Hannity interviewed Donald Trump: Aaron Blake, "Sean Hannity's Attempt to Coach Trump Backfires—Again," *Washington Post*, March 28, 2023, https://www.washingtonpost .com/politics/2023/03/28/sean-hannitys-attempt-coach -trump-backfires-again/.

134   "Except for day one": Colvin and Barrow, "Trump's Vow to Only Be a Dictator on 'Day One' Follows Growing Worry over His Authoritarian Rhetoric."

CHAPTER 7: **The Disloyal Opposition**

146   in the *Frontline* documentary: Jason M. Breslow, "The Opposition Strategy," *Frontline*, PBS, January 17, 2017, https://www.pbs.org /wgbh/frontline/interactive/divided-states-of-america-the-frontline -interviews/moments/the-opposition-strategy.html; also see https:// www.pbs.org/wgbh/frontline/documentary/divided-states-of-america /transcript/.

148 "that a party in opposition": Mark Trainer, "What's a 'Loyal Opposition,' and Why Does It Matter?," Share America, June 1, 2016, https://share.america.gov/why-loyal-opposition-matters.

151 "decidedly more confrontational": Henry Olsen, "Conservatives Owe Rush Limbaugh a Debt of Gratitude," *Washington Post*, February 4, 2020, https://www.washingtonpost.com /opinions/2020/02/04/two-cheers-rush-limbaugh/.

153 Buttigieg appeared on Fox: Brian Tyler Cohen, "Pete Buttigieg HUMILIATES Marjorie Taylor Greene on Fox," YouTube video, October 4, 2022, https://www.youtube.com /watch?v=JV7B5RWoeu4.

154 he appeared alongside: Brian Tyler Cohen, "Fed Up Pete Buttigieg Destroys Fox Host on His OWN SHOW," YouTube video, January 6, 2023, https://www.youtube.com/watch?v=gdTkqJF2zvs.

CHAPTER 8: **Poking Holes in Potatoes**

161 "The other reason": Though this was an interview with Marc conducted by me, some of his narrative also appeared in *The New Yorker* (Sue Halpern, "The First Defense Against Trump's Assault on Democracy," *The New Yorker*, April 13, 2022, https:// www.newyorker.com/news/persons-of-interest /the-first-defense-against-trumps-assault-on-democracy).

165 In 2018, forty-four House races were decided: Madison Hernandez, "Competitive Congressional Districts Decline," *Politico*, February 27, 2023, https://www.politico.com/newsletters /weekly-score/2023/02/27/competitive-congressional -districts-decline-00084506.

BRIAN TYLER COHEN is a progressive YouTuber, podcaster, and MSNBC contributor. He has over six million subscribers across all social media platforms, including a YouTube channel with two billion views and counting. His show, *No Lie with Brian Tyler Cohen*, has become a destination for the top names in politics, from Alexandria Ocasio-Cortez to Rachel Maddow to President Biden.